BOLLINGEN SERIES XCIX

ANALYTICAL PSYCHOLOGY

NOTES OF THE SEMINAR

GIVEN IN 1925 BY

C. G. JUNG

EDITED BY WILLIAM McGUIRE

BOLLINGEN SERIES XCIX

PRINCETON UNIVERSITY PRESS

THIS EDITION OF THE NOTES OF JUNG'S
SEMINARS IS BEING PUBLISHED IN THE
UNITED STATES OF AMERICA BY PRINCE-
TON UNIVERSITY PRESS, AND IN EN-
GLAND BY ROUTLEDGE LTD. IN THE
AMERICAN EDITION, THE VOLUMES OF
SEMINAR NOTES CONSTITUTE NUMBER
XCIX IN BOLLINGEN SERIES, SPON-
SORED BY BOLLINGEN FOUNDATION

The text here edited is that of the
original transcript prepared by Cary
F. de Angulo and privately issued in
multigraphed form by "members of
the class" and copyright 1926 by Dr.
C. G. Jung, Zurich

LIBRARY OF CONGRESS CATALOGING-IN-PUBLICATION DATA

JUNG, C. G. (CARL GUSTAV), 1875–1961.
ANALYTICAL PSYCHOLOGY : NOTES OF THE SEMINAR GIVEN IN 1925 /
BY C. G. JUNG ; EDITED BY WILLIAM MCGUIRE.
P. CM. — (BOLLINGEN SERIES ; 99)   INCLUDES INDEX.
ISBN 0-691-09897-2
ISBN 0-691-01918-5 (PBK.)
1. PSYCHOANALYSIS. I. MCGUIRE, WILLIAM, 1917–   . II. TITLE.
III. SERIES
BF 173.J666 1989   150.19'54—DC19   89-3533

FIRST PRINCETON/BOLLINGEN PAPERBACK PRINTING, 1991

5   7   9   10   8   6   4

PRINTED IN THE UNITED STATES OF AMERICA

TABLE OF CONTENTS

INTRODUCTION

This seminar, with its curiously synoptic title, was the first that Jung gave under relatively formal circumstances, and also the first that was recorded and multigraphed for the benefit of the growing body of his English-speaking students.[1] In 1925, Jung's fiftieth year, there was an evident need for an up-to-date presentation of the theory and method of analytical psychology for the educated lay public, and particularly for the English-speaking public. Eight years had passed since Jung had published a little book (his phrase), *Die Psychologie der unbewussten Prozesse*,[2] described in its subtitle as an *Ueberblick*, an overview. A translation, "The Psychology of the Unconscious Processes," was available only in the second edition of *Collected Papers of Analytical Psychology* (1917), a 520-page mélange of pre-Freudian, Freudian, and post-Freudian writings edited by the British psychiatrist Constance E. Long. That volume and the major long works *Psychology of the Unconscious* and *Psychological Types* constituted in 1925 the English-language reading list for the student of Jungian psychology. During April of that year, a month after Jung had begun the present seminar, he completed an extensively revised and improved popularization of the 1917 work, retitled *Das Unbewusste im normalen und kranken Seelenleben* (1926), which aimed "to give a rough idea of its subject and to provoke thought, but not to enter into all the details." Perhaps the experience of reviewing and discussing his system for the seminar had provoked the revision. Jung's 1926 overview reached its American and English public in 1928, translated by H. G. and C. F. Baynes as "The Unconscious in the Normal and Pathological Mind," which together with another work of a synoptic character, "The Relations

---

[1] For the informal seminars that Jung gave in 1912–1913(?), 1920, and 1923, and the more formal seminars (and ETH lectures) that he gave from 1928 to 1941, cf. *Dream Analysis*, introduction, pp. vii–xiii. (For abbreviated titles, see the list of abbreviations.) Another of the informal seminars opened at Swanage on July 25, barely a fortnight after the close of the present seminar, and on the day before Jung's fiftieth birthday. M. Esther Harding's longhand notes for this and the 1923 seminar survive.

[2] This had originated as a 36-page paper, "Neue Bahnen der Psychologie," in *Raschers Jahrbuch für schweizer Art und Kunst* (Zurich, 1912); translated as "New Paths in Psychology" in the 1st ed. of *Collected Papers on Analytical Psychology* (1916).

between the Ego and the Unconscious,"[3] composed the *Two Essays in Analytical Psychology*. The *Two Essays* continued for many years to be regarded as the introduction of choice.

*

On the opening day of this watershed year of 1925, Jung had been at the Grand Canyon of the Colorado River with a party of friends; a few days later he visited the Taos Pueblo, north of Santa Fe, New Mexico, and after that New Orleans, Chattanooga, and New York City.[4] He celebrated his fiftieth birthday, on July 26th, in Swanage, on the south coast of England. On the last day of the year, he was at Lake Kioga, in Uganda, preparing to embark on the journey by paddlewheel steamer down the Nile.[5] Throughout those venturesome travels, Jung's companions were English and American: in the Southwest, George F. Porter and Fowler McCormick, both of Chicago, and the Spanish-born Jaime de Angulo; in Africa, the English analyst H. Godwin Baynes, George Beckwith, an American, and an Englishwoman, Ruth Bailey. All except Miss Bailey were analysands of Jung at one time or another.

Of the twenty-seven recorded members of the 1925 seminar, thirteen were Americans, six were English, five (judging by our only evidence, their surnames) could be either, two were Swiss, one was German. Seven (all women) were Jungian analysts, of whom two were Swiss: Emma Jung, who had by this time begun to practice (her younger children were fourteen and eleven); and Tina Keller, who later moved to California with her husband Adolf Keller, a Protestant pastor early drawn to psychoanalysis—he attended the Weimar Congress in 1911. The Americans included the New York troika—M. Esther Harding, Eleanor Bertine, and Kristine Mann, all physicians. Harding, from Shropshire in the west of England, had qualified at the London School of Medicine for Women in 1914. Her colleague Constance Long introduced her to *Psychology of the Unconscious*, newly

[3] Originally a 27-page lecture, in 1916, to the Zurich School of Analytical Psychology, first published in a French translation, "La structure de l'inconscient," *Archives de psychologie* (Geneva), XVI (1916). An English translation appeared in *Collected Papers*, 2nd ed. (1917). It first appeared in German, much revised and expanded, as *Die Beziehungen zwischen dem Ich and dem Unbewussten* (1928), the source of the translation in *Two Essays on Analytical Psychology*.

[4] William McGuire, "Jung in America, 1924–1925," *Spring*, 1978, pp. 37–53.

[5] Barbara Hannah, *Jung, His Life and Work: A Biographical Memoir* (New York, 1976), p. 176.

published in the Beatrice Hinkle translation. In the 1920s Harding began visiting Zurich for personal analysis with Jung and there encountered Mann and Bertine. Mann had left a career as an English professor to work for an M.D. at the Cornell University Medical College in New York, where Eleanor Bertine was a classmate. Both earned their degrees in 1913. In the 1920s they began analysis with Jung during trips to Switzerland, and in 1924 they decided to join Harding in an analytic practice in the States. The three women founded the Jungian community in New York City: the Analytical Psychology Club (and its incomparable library named for Kristine Mann), the C. G. Jung Institute, and the C. G. Jung Foundation.[6]

The other American, Elida Evans, had not been part of the Jungian circle in New York, or so it would appear. In 1915 she had been in Zurich for analysis with Maria Moltzer, and in 1920 Jung introduced her book on child psychology. In those same years, as a lay analyst in New York, she had assisted Smith Ely Jelliffe, a psychoanalyst who had friendly relations with both Jung and Freud.[7] The other analyst recorded in the seminar, Dr. Helen Shaw, is an obscure figure. An articulate member of the Dream Analysis seminar, she is said to have had professional ties with both England and Australia.[8]

Another category embraces those seminarians who were, in some degree, literary. The American writer Charles Roberts Aldrich, if we may judge by his comments in the seminar, was an intellectual of more than usual sophistication. He helped Jung revise the English text of the lectures on psychology and education he delivered in London during the spring of 1924. When Aldrich left Zurich to return home to California, he gave Jung his dog, Joggi, who was Jung's familiar for years afterward and had his place in the consulting room.[9] In 1931, Aldrich published in C. K. Ogden's International Library of Psychology, Philosophy, and Scientific Method a learned book, *The Primitive Mind and Modern Civilization*, which had an introduction by the anthropologist Bronislaw Malinowski, a foreword by Jung,[10] and

---

[6] Doreen B. Lee, "The C. G. Jung Foundation: The First Twenty-one Years," *Quadrant*, 16: 2 (Fall 1983), pp. 57–61.

[7] John C. Burnham and William McGuire, *Jelliffe: American Psychoanalyst and Physician, & His Correspondence with Sigmund Freud and C. G. Jung* (Chicago, 1983), index, s.v. Evans. Cf. Jung's foreword to Evans's *The Problem of the Nervous Child*, CW 18, pars. 1793–94.

[8] Information from Dr. Joseph Henderson. Cf. *Dream Analysis*, index, s.v. Shaw.

[9] Jung to Aldrich, 5 Jan. 1931, in *Jung: Letters*, vol. 1, p. 80; Elizabeth Shepley Sergeant, "Doctor Jung: A Portrait in 1931," *Jung Speaking*, pp. 51–52.

[10] CW 18, pars. 1296–99.

a dedication to the memory of George F. Porter, who had been with Jung in New Mexico and died a suicide in 1927. Aldrich's career also ended with his sudden death, in 1933, which he had predicted to the day though in perfect health.[11] Another American, the poet Leonard Bacon, had come to Zurich in 1925 for analysis with Jung, who invited him to join the seminar.[12] That year's experiences were reflected in a volume of poems, *Animula Vagula* (1926). Bacon's subsequent career as a poet, critic, and translator was distinguished; he was awarded the Pulitzer Prize for poetry in 1940.

Still another literary American, Elizabeth Shepley Sergeant, may have been one of Jung's first, or even *the* first, analysand from the United States. In her twenties, while traveling in Europe with an aunt, Sergeant suffered some form of nervous disorder and was treated at a sanitarium in Zurich during the winter of 1904–1905. According to family lore, it may have been then that she was first analyzed by Jung.[13] At that time, though Jung had not met Freud, he had begun using the Freudian method, sometimes combined with the association test, at the Burghölzli Hospital—as he had done in the case of Sabina Spielrein.[14] Sergeant became a well-known newspaperwoman; she was a correspondent for *The New Republic* during the First World War and was wounded while visiting a battlefield near Rheims. While hospitalized in Paris for six months, she was visited by such friends as Walter Lippmann, Simon Flexner, and William C. Bullitt.[15] During her long career as both journalist and literary critic, her subjects included Robert Frost, Willa Cather, William Alanson White, Paul Robeson, H. L. Mencken, and many others. Among several pieces about Jung, a "portrait" that Sergeant published in 1931 presents a picture of him at a seminar meeting she attended:

> When, on Wednesday morning at eleven, . . . Doctor Jung enters the long room at the Psychological Club where his Seminar is held, smiling with a deep friendliness at this or that face, the brown portfolio which he hugs to his side seems to be the repos-

[11] *The New York Times,* 9 April 1933, IV, 7: 5.

[12] Bacon, *Semi-centennial: Some of the Life and Part of the Opinions of Leonard Bacon* (New York, 1939), p. 182.

[13] Linda H. Davis, *Onward and Upward: A Biography of Katherine S. White* (New York, 1987), pp. 27–28. Katherine S. White, an editor of *The New Yorker,* was Sergeant's younger sister.

[14] Jung to Freud, 23 Oct. 1906, *Freud/Jung*; Aldo Carotenùto, *A Secret Symmetry: Sabina Spielrein between Jung and Freud* (New York, 2nd ed., 1984), pp. 139ff.

[15] Sergeant, *Shadow Shapes: The Journal of a Wounded Woman* (Boston, 1920).

itory of this joint account—the collective account of a small international group whose common interest is the psyche. An involuntary hush falls on the room as Jung himself stands quiet and grave for a moment, looking down at his manuscript as a sailor might look at his compass, relating it to the psychological winds and waves whose impact he has felt on his passage from the door. The hush in the assembly means not only reverence but intense expectation. What world adventure shall we have today with this creative thinker? What question, like the stroke of a bronze bell, will he leave ringing in our minds? What drastic vision of our age will he give us that will help us to lose our sense of problems, subjective and oppressive, and move into a more universal and objective realm?[16]

Jung would have learned of the anthropologist Paul Radin's research on American Indian ethnography and religion from Cary and Jaime de Angulo, who had known Radin in California before 1920. In that year, Radin went to England to work at Cambridge University under the anthropologist W.H.R. Rivers, lecturing, teaching, and pursuing research.[17] He was still in Cambridge five years later when Jung, perhaps stimulated by his recent experiences with Jaime de Angulo and Mountain Lake at the Taos Pueblo, invited Radin to come to Zurich and talk to him and his pupils about the religion of American Indians. (It is said that Jung paid for the trip.) Radin talked informally to the members of the Psychological Club, participated in the seminar, and formed a lifetime friendship with Jung. A fellow anthropologist wrote that "in these years, aside from Rivers, it was C. G. Jung in Zurich who provided intellectual grist to a man who was already much interested in comparative religion and literature. That Radin was never a Jungian goes without saying. Perhaps his very contact with Jung's cultivated but mystical mind served to reinforce Radin's skeptical rationalism and alienated him from explorations in at least the murkier depths of the unconscious."[18] In the 1940s Radin (never renouncing his Marxist view of society) became an influential adviser to the Bollingen Foundation, whose support enabled him to continue his writing. He lectured at the Eranos confer-

[16] "Doctor Jung: A Portrait," *Harper's*, May, 1931; in *Jung Speaking*, pp. 52–53.
[17] Cora Du Bois, "Paul Radin: An Appreciation," in *Culture in History: Essays in Honor of Paul Radin* (New York, 1960), p. xiii.
[18] Ibid.

ences and collaborated with Jung and Karl Kerényi on a book about the archetype of the Trickster.

While in Zurich, Radin and his wife, Rose, discovered acquaintances from California: Kenneth Robertson and his wife, Sidney. Robertson, who had studied psychological testing under L. M. Terman at Stanford University, had gone to Europe intending to train as a lay analyst. In Paris, at the bookshop called Shakespeare & Co., he discovered a copy of *Psychology of the Unconscious* and forthwith wrote Jung, who invited him to come and train in Zurich—as it transpired, to work analytically with Toni Wolff and attend the seminar. Sidney Robertson, on her part, worked with Kristine Mann and also sat in the seminar, silently. (She remembered, in a recent interview, that Hermann Hesse and Richard Strauss each, also silently, dropped in on a session.) Jung, who had set young Sidney Robertson to work correcting and typing his lectures on psychology and education, pronounced her husband unanalyzable. The Robertsons, nevertheless, along with some of the other seminarians, followed Jung to Swanage for the Dreams and Symbolism seminar in late July. Then they went home to Oakland, where Robertson for a time tried to make it as a lay analyst, then gave up and took a job with the post office. Over the years, nonetheless, he preserved a friendly rapport with the Jungian pioneers in the Bay Area, the Whitneys and the Gibbs.[19]

Two literary Englishwomen: Charlotte A. Baynes and Joan Corrie. Baynes (apparently unrelated to the analyst H. G. Baynes) was later to publish a book that Jung quoted often in his writings on alchemy: *A Coptic Gnostic Treatise, Contained in the Codex Brucianus* (1933). When she lectured at the Eranos conference of 1937, she was identified as an anthropologist, an Oxonian scholar of Gnosticism, and an O.B.E. We know that she also worked on an archaeological dig in Jerusalem. Joan Corrie had been active in England as a pupil of Jung's for some years. After attending the 1925 seminar, she wrote a small book that was the first presentation of his ideas for the general reader: *ABC of Jung's Psychology* (London and New York, 1927), which includes diagrams and quotations from the 1925 seminar.[20]

One literary German: Oskar A. H. Schmitz, a novelist, a critic of the contemporary European scene, noted for his wit, and a student

[19] Personal communication from Sidney (Mrs. Henry) Cowell. After divorcing Robertson, she married the American composer Henry Cowell. She continued a friendship with Radin.

[20] Some of the extracts do not occur in Cary de Angulo's transcript; in the present edition these are given as addenda.

of depth psychology and yoga. Though nearly three years older than Jung, Schmitz considered himself Jung's pupil—and he was surely the senior one. He had introduced Jung to Count Hermann Keyserling, the founder of the "School of Wisdom" in Darmstadt, where Jung occasionally lectured, and where in 1923 he met Richard Wilhelm, his master in the art of the *I Ching*.[21] Schmitz had an evident urge to practice as an analyst, and may have done so: he once wrote Jung asking his advice regarding fees and hours.[22] After Schmitz's sudden death, in 1931, Jung wrote a posthumous tribute by way of a foreword to "The Tale of the Otter," a work of Schmitz's that had arisen from an experience of the unconscious.[23]

A somewhat unclassifiable American member of the seminar was Elisabeth Houghton, the daughter of Alanson Bigelow Houghton, the United States ambassador to Germany from 1921 to 1925 and to the United Kingdom from 1925 to 1929. She was a cousin of Katherine Houghton Hepburn, an early activist for Planned Parenthood. According to her mother's London diary (which has nothing to say about Zurich or psychology),[24] the girl was sixteen at the time she attended the seminar—that would necessarily have been at Jung's invitation. Elisabeth Houghton, in later life, devoted herself to the Red Cross and other good works but did not remain in the Jungian orbit.

*

Cary F. de Angulo was responsible for the existence of this record of Jung's seminar. As Cary F. Baynes, her name is widely known for her translation of the *I Ching*; and as a translator and friend of Jung she was a central figure in the world of analytical psychology. The latter form of her name is so familiar that it is easier to use it now.

Cary Baynes may have been the only member of the seminar (perhaps of *any* of the seminars) who did not go to Zurich because of an

[21] Gerhard Wehr, *Jung: A Biography*, tr. D. M. Weeks (Boston and London, 1987), p. 6. Cf. Jung, "Marriage as a Psychological Relationship" (1925), CW 17, pars. 324ff.; and "Mind and Earth" (1927), CW 10, pars. 49ff. See also *Sinnsuche oder Psychoanalyse: Briefwechsel Graf Hermann Keyserling—Oskar A. H. Schmitz aus den Tagen der Schule der Weisheit* (Darmstadt, 1970), Register, s.v. Jung.

[22] *Jung: Letters*, vol. 1, p. 54 (20 Sept. 1928).

[23] CW 18, pars. 171ff.

[24] Adelaide Louise Houghton, *The London Years 1925–1929* (New York, 1963; privately published), entries for 28 Oct. 1925, 21 Feb. 1926. / Personal communication from James R. Houghton.

interest in Jung, clinical or otherwise. But best to begin at the beginning.[25]

Mexico City was her birthplace, in 1883. Her father, Rudolph Fink, a native of Darmstadt, was building a railroad to Veracruz. Cary and her older sister, Henri, grew up in Louisville, Kentucky, their mother's home town. At Vassar College (A.B., 1906), Cary excelled in a course in argumentation taught by a professor of English, Kristine Mann. In 1911, she earned an M.D. degree at the Johns Hopkins University. The previous year she had married another Johns Hopkins M.D., Jaime de Angulo, of Spanish origin, transplanted to the Big Sur coast of California. Cary never practiced medicine; her husband practiced only as a medical officer in the U.S. Army, and instead made a career as an anthropologist. He was a gifted student of American Indian languages. In 1921, Cary left de Angulo. She and her three-year-old daughter Ximena went to Europe with her college teacher Kristine Mann, by then a physician and an adherent of Jung's psychology. Having settled in Zurich, Cary was persuaded by Mann to study with Jung. In summer 1923, she attended Jung's seminar at Polzeath, in Cornwall. By 1925, when she recorded the present seminar, she was thoroughly grounded in the system of analytical psychology. Her sister Henri (an artist who had been married to a man named Zinno) had joined her in Zurich and studied alongside her.

Jung's assistant at that time was the British analyst H. Godwin Baynes, M.D., who had translated *Psychological Types*, and who traveled with Jung to East Africa during the winter of 1925–1926. He married Cary de Angulo the following year, and while living in England they collaborated as translators of Jung's *Contributions to Analytical Psychology* and *Two Essays on Analytical Psychology* (both published in 1928). A year in the United States followed: Cary and her daughter lived in Carmel, and Baynes had an analytical practice there and in Berkeley, where he met young Joseph Henderson and pointed him toward his career as an analyst.

Again in Zurich, Cary was asked by Jung to translate Richard Wilhelm's German version of the *I Ching*, which had come out in 1924. Wilhelm was to have supervised the translation, but his death in 1930 intervened. Meanwhile, Cary Baynes translated *The Secret of the Golden Flower*—Wilhelm's rendering of the Chinese text, with Jung's

---

[25] Biographical data from Ximena de Angulo Roelli. See also W. McGuire, *Bollingen: An Adventure in Collecting the Past* (Princeton, 1982), index, s.v. "Baynes, Cary F.," and p. 330.

xiv

commentary (1931). After Cary and H. G. Baynes were divorced, she continued to live in Zurich, rejoined by her sister, Henri Zinno. During the 1930s, Cary worked on the *I Ching* translation, translated (with W. S. Dell) *Modern Man in Search of a Soul* (1933), attended Jung's seminars, and helped Olga Froebe-Kapteyn manage the Eranos conferences in Ascona. She was active in the Psychological Club, and, as an associate said, "tried to restrain some of the excessive intriguing and to keep things on an objective plane." The Baynes-Zinno house was a meeting-place for American and English as well as European followers and students of Jung. Jane and Joseph Wheelwright lived there while going through analysis. At Jung's request, Cary helped, as a companion, with James Joyce's daughter Lucia during a psychotic episode.

In the words of her daughter Ximena, Cary Baynes "never 'qualified' as an analyst, never worked analytically, and never had patients, in the sense that she never accepted any regular relationship of analyst to patient or any fees, but all through her mature life there was an endless stream of people coming to consult her. When asked why she didn't set up as an analyst, she would always give two reasons: one, that she had 'no contact with the collective unconscious,' and, two, that Jung had said that no one should engage in analysis who was not backed by a very strong relationship to a partner, to keep him from being sucked into his patients' problems, as it were, and from losing his grip on reality."[26] And Joseph Henderson has observed that "the two sisters had, one might say, a symbiotic relationship. Cary was the serious leader of any discussion, while Henri provided the humor, hospitality, and feminine charm. Cary had a formidable grasp of Jungian theory and applied it consciously with great skill. You might say Henri *was* her experience of the unconscious. Henri lived close to the edge of it, and her painting and sculpture were purely archetypal."[27]

In the late 1930s, the two sisters returned to the United States. Cary had met Mary and Paul Mellon at Olga Froebe-Kapteyn's villa near Ascona, and when Mary Mellon set up the first Bollingen Foundation in 1940, its office was at Cary's house in Washington, Connecticut. Cary was a member of its board and Ximena de Angulo was its first editor. Wartime circumstances forced the Foundation's dissolution in 1942, but it was revived in 1945, and Cary accompanied its

[26] Personal communication (11 Jan. 1978).
[27] Personal communication (29 Jan. 1978).

associate editor, John D. Barrett, when he attended his first Eranos conference in 1946. After Mary Mellon's sudden death that September, Barrett, as head of the Foundation and editor of its Bollingen Series, continued to rely on Cary as one of his most prudent advisers. Her translation of the *I Ching* appeared as Bollingen Series XIX in 1950, and she later translated *Change: Eight Lectures on the I Ching*, by Richard Wilhelm's son Hellmut (Bollingen Series LXII, 1960).

After her sister Henri died, in 1970, Cary lived in Ascona. She was intellectually active until her death, in 1977—having been the eldest surviving member of the close circle of pupils and friends that had formed around Jung in the 1920s. "She probably did more for me than most analysts," Jane Wheelwright said, after Cary's death. "I don't know why she couldn't have been an analyst. She was the Rock of Gibraltar."[28]

*

In the editing of the transcript, nothing has been omitted. Silent changes chiefly concern punctuation, spelling, grammar, and clarity. Speculative alterations are in brackets and, if necessary, are commented on in a footnote. The dates of the lectures have been supplied; see note 1 to Lecture 2. The material that follows Lecture 16 is taken to be part of that lecture; see note 5 to Lecture 16. The diagrams have been redrawn. Passages that were adapted in *Memories, Dreams, Reflections* are noted.

Another multigraphed version of the transcript of this seminar exists, retyped (in the same number of pages), undated, and unrevised, though many typographical errors were corrected and the diagrams were redrawn. For the present edition a copy was consulted through the courtesy of the Virginia Allen Detloff Library of the C. G. Jung Institute of San Francisco. An index compiled by Mary Briner, issued in multigraph in 1939, covers the Notes of the English Seminars from 1925 to Winter 1934: namely, *Analytical Psychology, Dream Analysis, Interpretation of Visions*, and *Kundalini Yoga*. The index in the present volume draws upon Briner's treatment of conceptual terms.

WILLIAM McGUIRE

[28] Personal communication (Feb. 1978).

ACKNOWLEDGMENTS

I am grateful to the following persons who replied to my questions arising from the text of the seminar, or regarding the members, or who were helpful in other ways: Doris Albrecht and Peggy Brooks, of the Kristine Mann Library; Joan Alpert, of the Virginia Allen Detloff Library; Gerhard Adler, Helen H. Bacon, Paula D. Black, G. W. Bowersock, Clarence F. Brown, Mark R. Cohen, Sidney Cowell, Gordon A. Craig, Dorothy Salisbury Davis, Gui de Angulo, Violet de Laszlo, Edward F. Edinger, Michael Fordham, Joseph Frank, Marie-Louise von Franz, Felix Gilbert, Joseph Henderson, James R. Houghton, Aniela Jaffé, Lorenz Jung, James Kirsch, Frances Lange, Victor Lange, Phyllis W. Lehmann, Verena Maag, Ximena de Angulo Roelli, Jerome Ross, Mary Sacharoff-Fast Wolf, Sonu Shamdasani, John Shearman, Jane Lincoln Taylor, Jane Wheelwright, and Joseph Wheelwright.

W. M.

MEMBERS OF THE SEMINAR

The following list accounts for persons whose names appear in the original multigraphed transcript; others may have attended whose names were not recorded. In the original transcript only surnames (with Mr., etc.) are given. (No register has survived.) Here, the full names, country of residence, etc., have been supplied insofar as possible. An asterisk indicates a person who, according to present knowledge, was or later became an analytical psychologist. The column at right gives the number of the first seminar meeting (lecture) at which a member's name turns up. Also see the index of this volume.

Aldrich, Mr. Charles Roberts (U.S.)	Lecture 5
Bacon, Mr. Leonard (U.S.)	Lecture 7
Baynes, Miss Charlotte A. (U.K.)	Lecture 7
*Bertine, Dr. Eleanor (U.S.)	Appendix to Lecture 16
Bond, Dr.	Lecture 15
Corrie, Miss Joan (U.K.)	Lecture 9
de Angulo, Dr. Cary Fink (later Baynes) (U.S.)	Lecture 2
Dunham, Mrs.	Lecture 2
*Evans, Mrs. Elida (U.S.)	Lecture 9
Gordon, Dr. Mary (U.K.)	Lecture 2
*Harding, Dr. M. Esther (U.K./U.S.)	Lecture 6
Henty, Miss Dorothy (U.K.)	Lecture 9
Hincks, Miss	Lecture 9
Houghton, Miss Elisabeth (U.S.)	Lecture 13
*Jung, Mrs. Emma (Switzerland)	Appendix to Lecture 16
*Keller, Mrs. Tina (Switzerland)	Lecture 9
*Mann, Dr. Kristine (U.S.)	Lecture 2
Radin, Dr. Paul (U.S.)	Lecture 13
Raevsky, Miss	Lecture 15
Robertson, Mr. Kenneth (U.S.)	Lecture 9
Schmitz, Mr. Oskar A. H. (Germany)	Lecture 15
Sergeant, Miss Elizabeth Shepley (U.S.)	Lecture 15
*Shaw, Dr. Helen (U.K./Australia)	Lecture 2
Taylor, Miss Ethel (U.K.)	Lecture 13
Ward, Dr.	Lecture 9
Zinno, Mrs. Henri Fink (U.S.)	Lecture 6

LIST OF ABBREVIATIONS

B.S. = Bollingen Series. New York and Princeton.

CW = The Collected Works of C. G. Jung. Edited by Gerhard Adler, Michael Fordham, and Herbert Read; William McGuire, Executive Editor; translated by R.F.C. Hull. New York and Princeton (Bollingen Series XX) and London, 1953–1983. 21 vols.

Dream Analysis. Notes of the Seminar Given in 1928–1930 by C. G. Jung. Edited by William McGuire. Princeton (Bollingen Series XCIX:1) and London, 1984.

Freud/Jung = *The Freud/Jung Letters.* Edited by William McGuire; translated by Ralph Manheim and R.F.C. Hull. Princeton (Bollingen Series XCIV) and London, 1974. New edition, Cambridge, Massachusetts, 1988.

Jung: Letters = *C. G. Jung: Letters.* Selected and edited by Gerhard Adler in collaboration with Aniela Jaffé; translations by R.F.C. Hull. Princeton (Bollingen Series XCV) and London, 1973, 1975. 2 vols.

Jung: Word and Image = *C. G. Jung: Word and Image.* Edited by Aniela Jaffé; translated by Krishna Winston. Princeton (Bollingen Series XCVII:2) and London, 1979.

Jung Speaking = *C. G. Jung Speaking: Interviews and Encounters.* Edited by William McGuire and R.F.C. Hull. Princeton (Bollingen Series XCVII) and London (abridged), 1977.

MDR = *Memories, Dreams, Reflections by C. G. Jung.* Recorded and edited by Aniela Jaffé; translated by Richard and Clara Winston. New York and London, 1963. (The editions are differently paginated; double page references are given, first to the New York edition.)

SE = The Standard Edition of the Complete Psychological Works of Sigmund Freud. Translated under the general editorship of James Strachey, in collaboration with Anna Freud, assisted by Alix Strachey and Alan Tyson. London and New York, 1953–1974. 24 vols.

Spring: An Annual of Archetypal Psychology and Jungian Thought. New York and Zurich; now Dallas.

Types = *Psychological Types.* CW 6 (1971).

Zarathustra = *Nietzsche's "Zarathustra."* Notes of the Seminar Given in 1934–1939 by C. G. Jung. Edited by James L. Jarrett. Princeton (Bollingen Series XCIX:2) and London, 1988. 2 vols.

FOREWORD

The multigraphing of these notes has been done at the request of members of the class whose wish it was to have some permanent record of the lectures, even if only in schematic form. In contrast to the fullness and vividness of the lectures, the notes are disappointingly "thin," but as I could find no way of counteracting this defect, I must invoke the good will of the class and ask that the notes be looked upon merely as an outline serviceable to the memory.

For the sake of convenience of form, I have presented the lectures, questions, and discussions for the most part as though in the words of the speakers, but in point of fact, only the written questions are literally so exact. For the rest, I have not tried to do more than cover as completely as possible the sense of what was said.

The copies of the diagrams are not my work, but are the valuable contribution of another member of the class. Others still have helped me greatly in supplementing the material and in the work of correction. The whole has been reviewed and corrected by Dr. Jung.

Zurich, November 29th, 1925.   CARY F. DE ANGULO

ANALYTICAL PSYCHOLOGY

LECTURE 1

23 March 1925

Dr. Jung:

No one seriously interested in analytical psychology can fail to have been struck with the astonishing width of the field embraced by it, and so I have thought it would be useful to all of us if, in the course of these lectures, we could obtain a view of that field. At the beginning, I would like to give you a brief sketch of the development of my own conceptions from the time I first became interested in problems of the unconscious. As on previous occasions, you can assist me greatly if you contribute written questions, permitting me to select the ones suitable for discussion.

*

In 1896 something happened to me that served as an impetus for my future life. A thing of this sort is always to be expected in a man's life—that is to say, his family history alone is never the key to his creative achievements. The thing that started me off in my interest in psychology was the case of the fifteen-and-a-half-year-old girl whose case I have described in the *Collected Papers*,[1] as the first contribution to that series. This girl was a somnambulist, and it was discovered by her sisters that they could obtain extraordinary answers to questions put to her when she was in the sleeping state: in other words, she was found to be a medium. I was impressed with the fact that, notwithstanding appearances, there must be a hidden life of the mind manifesting itself only in trance or in sleep. A little hypnosis would send this girl into a trance from which she would later awake as from sleep. During the trance several personalities would manifest themselves; and, little by little, I found I could call up by suggestion one person-

---

[1] "On the Psychology and Pathology of So-called Occult Phenomena" (tr. M. D. Eder), in *Collected Papers on Analytical Psychology*, ed. Constance E. Long (New York and London, 1916; 2nd ed., 1917), pp. 1–93. (CW 1, pars. 1ff., tr. R.F.C. Hull.) Cf. *MDR*, pp. 106f./109f.

ality or another. In short, I found I could have a formative influence on them.

Of course I became deeply interested in all these things and began to try to explain them, something I could not do as I was only twenty-one at the time, and quite ignorant along these lines. I said to myself, however, that there must be some world behind the conscious world, and that it was this world with which the girl was in contact. I began to study the literature of spiritism but could find no satisfaction there. Then I turned to philosophy, always seeking for a possible clue to these strange phenomena.

I was a student of medicine at the time and deeply interested in it, but also deeply interested in philosophy. Finally in my searching I came to Schopenhauer and Hartmann.[2] From Schopenhauer I got a very enlightening point of view. His fundamental standpoint is that the will as a blind urge to existence is aimless; it simply "happened to the creative will to make the world." This is his position in *The World as Will and Idea*. However, in *Will in Nature*[3] he drifts into a teleological attitude, though this is in direct opposition to his original thesis, something, be it said, which not infrequently happens to a philosopher. In this latter work he assumes that there is direction in the creating will, and this point of view I took as mine. My first conception of the libido then was not that it was a formless stream so to speak, but that it was archetypal in character. That is to say, libido never comes up from the unconscious in a formless state, but always in images. Using a figure of speech, the ore brought up from the mine of the unconscious is always crystallized.

Out of this reading of Schopenhauer, I got a tentative explanation of the possible psychology of the case I was studying; that is, I thought the personifications might be the result of this image-forming tendency of the libido. If I suggested a given person to the girl during her unconscious states, she would act that person out, and her answers to questions would come in a manner characteristic of the person suggested. From this I became convinced of the tendency of the unconscious material to flow into definite moulds. This gave a clue, too, to the disintegration of personality. In dementia praecox, for example, there is an independent working of the different parts of the psyche, but there is generally nothing vague about the differ-

[2] For Jung's discovery of Eduard von Hartmann (1842–1906) and Arthur Schopenhauer (1788–1860) while a medical student at Basel University, see *The Zofingia Lectures* (1896–1899; CW, suppl. vol. A), index, s.vv.

[3] *Die Welt als Wille und Vorstellung* (1818); *Über den Willen in der Natur* (1836).

4

ent parts; the voices that are heard are the voices of definite individuals, of particular persons, and that is why they are so real. In the same way a spiritualist will always claim a high degree of individuality and personal character for his "spirits." At this time I thought that after all there might be ghosts.

My ideas of the unconscious, then, first became enlightened through Schopenhauer and Hartmann. Hartmann, having the advantage of living in a later period than Schopenhauer, formulates the latter's ideas in a more modern way. He assumes what he calls the *Weltgrund* to be the unconscious spirit or entity which has creative efficiency, and this he calls the unconscious, but adds to it mind.[4] He uses mind here in a different sense from that in which Schopenhauer uses it. Schopenhauer opposes mind to the blind creating will. By some unforeseen accident man came into possession of a conscious mirror of the universe, namely mind, and through this he knows the evilness of the world and deliberately withdraws therefrom, thus putting himself into opposition with the creating will. In Schopenhauer's conception mind belongs to man alone and is not connected with the *Weltgrund* or *unbewusster Geist*. I held, following Hartmann, that our unconscious is not meaningless but contains a mind. After I had taken this position I found much contradictory evidence, and so the pendulum swung back and forth. At one time it seemed as though there must be some thread of purpose running through the unconscious, at another I was convinced there was none.

At this point the medium "ran out," that is to say, she began to cheat and I gave up all connection with her. I had observed her for a period of two years, and had given myself up to a study of the detailed phenomena she presented, striving to get them into harmony with natural science. But I know now that I overlooked the most important feature of the situation, namely my connection with it. The girl had of course fallen deeply in love with me, and of this I was fairly ignorant and quite ignorant of the part it played in her psychology.

In her trances she had formulated for herself a very superior character, that of an older woman of great spiritual beauty. She herself, in reality a very silly and superficial girl, could find no other way of expressing this unconscious urge within herself to be different save through the spiritualistic setting, and the acting out of the character she found there. Her family, originally one of the old families of

---

[4] *Philosophie des Unbewussten* (1869); tr., *Philosophy of the Unconscious* (1931).

5

Basel, had gone into rather complete decay, both financially and culturally. The girl herself could be described as a "midinette." When she met me she found me interested in all the sides of life she craved, but from which she had been cut off by fate. Had I known then what I know now I could have understood the struggle she went through in order to express the best in her through this person of the trance, but as it was I could only see her as a silly little girl who began to do something very ugly, namely to cheat for the sake of impressing me and others. I only saw her as a person who had ruined her reputation and spoiled her chances in life; but, as a matter of fact, through this very act of cheating she forced her way back into reality. She gave up the mediumistic séances and all of that fantastic side of her gradually faded out of existence. Later she went to Paris and entered the atelier of a famous dress-maker. In a relatively short time she had an establishment of her own and was most successful, making extraordinarily beautiful and original clothes. I saw her in Paris during this period, but practically all of the mediumistic experiences had faded from her mind. Then she contracted tuberculosis, but would not admit that she really had the disease. A few weeks before her death it was as though she were making a regression further and further back in her life, till finally she was about two years old, and then she died.[5]

She is an example of the general psychological law that in order to advance to a higher stage of development, we often have to commit some mistake which apparently is so terrible as to threaten ruin to our lives. The dishonesty of the girl had the ultimate result of breaking up the mediumistic séances, and then she was able to live out in reality the character she had developed for herself in the unconscious. She first worked up in the spirit world what she wanted in reality, but then the spirit world had to decay before she could get rid of the transcendental elements. Her life is an illustration of the principle of enantiodromia[6] because starting with the thing that was most evil in her, namely her willingness to cheat and her general weakness and silliness, she passed by steady progression to the opposite pole where she was expressing the best that was in her.

After this period, which contains the origin of all my ideas, I found

---

[5] The girl was Hélène Preiswerk, Jung's first cousin. Cf. Stefanie Zumstein-Preiswerk, *C. G. Jung's Medium: Die Geschichte der Helly Preiswerk* (Munich, 1975), and summary in James Hillman, "Some Early Background to Jung's Ideas: Notes on *C. G. Jung's Medium . . .*," *Spring*, 1976, pp. 123–36.

[6] See *Psychological Types* (CW 6), Def. 18.

Nietzsche.[7] I was twenty-four when I read *Zarathustra*. I could not understand it, but it made a profound impression upon me, and I felt an analogy between it and the girl in some peculiar way. Later, of course, I found that *Zarathustra* was written from the unconscious and is a picture of what that man should be. If Zarathustra [the protagonist] had come through as a reality for Nietzsche instead of remaining in his "spirit world," the intellectual Nietzsche would have had to go. But this feat of realization, Nietzsche could not accomplish. It was more than his brain could master.

[handwritten margin note: two sides to Nietzsche the intellectual cns vcs Zarathustra]

All of this time I was continuing as a student of medicine, but I was keeping up my reading in philosophy on the side. When I was twenty-five, I passed my final examination in medicine. It had been my intention to specialize in internal medicine. I was deeply interested in physiological chemistry, and had the chance of becoming the assistant of a famous man.[8] Nothing was further from my mind then than psychiatry. One reason for this was the fact that my father, as a minister, was connected with the cantonal insane asylum and very much interested in psychiatry. Like all sons, I knew that whatever my father was interested in was wrong, and so I avoided it as carefully as I could. I had never read even one book having to do with psychiatry, but when it came time for me to take my final examinations, I got a textbook and started in to investigate this idiotic subject. The book was by Krafft-Ebing.[9] I said to myself, "Anybody so foolish as to write a textbook on this subject is bound to explain himself in a preface," so I turned to the preface. By the time I had finished the first page I was on edge with interest. By the time I was halfway down the second page, I had such a beating of the heart I could hardly go on. "By God," I said, "that is what I will be, a psychiatrist." I passed first in my examinations, and great was the surprise of all my friends when I made the announcement that I would be a psychiatrist. None of them knew that in that book of Krafft-Ebing's I had found the clue to the riddle I was seeking to solve. Their comment was, "Well, we always thought you were crazy, and now we know it!" I told nobody that I intended to work out the unconscious phenomena of the psy-

---

[7] *The Zofingia Lectures*, index, s.v. Cf. Jung's later seminar on *Also Sprach Zarathustra* (1934–1939), in the present series, with an introduction by James L. Jarrett discussing Jung's interest in Nietzsche.

[8] Friedrich von Müller. Cf. *MDR*, p. 107/110.

[9] Richard von Krafft-Ebing, *Lehrbuch von Psychiatrie auf klinische Grundlage*, 4th ed. (1890); tr., *Test-Book of Insanity Based on Clinical Observations* (1904). Cf. *MDR*, p. 108/110. Jung's library contains the 4th German ed.

choses, but that was my determination. I wanted to catch the intruders in the mind—the intruders that make people laugh when they should not laugh, and cry when they should not cry. When I developed my association tests[10] it was the defects that the tests brought out that held my interest. I made careful note of the places where people could not achieve the experiments, and out of these observations I came to my theory of autonomous complexes as being the cause of the blockage in libido flow. Freud at the same time was evolving his conception of the complex.

In 1900 I read Freud's *Dream Interpretation*.[11] I put it aside as something whose significance I did not fully grasp. Then I returned to it in 1903 and found in it the connection with my own theories.

[10] "Studies in Word Association" (1904–1909), in CW 2. Jung's correspondence with Freud was inaugurated by his gift of a copy of the first volume of *Diagnostische Assoziationstudien* by him and others. Among its contents, "Psychoanalysis and Association Experiments" (1906) was Jung's first significant publication on the subject of psychoanalysis. See *Freud/Jung*, 1 F (11 Apr. 1906).

[11] *The Interpretation of Dreams* (1900; SE, vols. IV–V). Cf. *MDR*, pp. 146f./144. Cf. also Jung's report, dated 25 Jan. 1901, on Freud's *Über den Traum* (1901; a summary of the 1900 work), in CW 18, pars. 841ff. Jung's first citation of *The Interpretation of Dreams* occurs in the "Occult Phenomena" monograph, 1902; see CW 1, pars. 97 and 133.

LECTURE 2

30 March 1925[1]

QUESTIONS AND DISCUSSION

Dr. Shaw's question: "Could such a case as the girl you spoke of last Monday, if properly analyzed, be helped to find her true self, something midway between her superior unconscious personification and her inferior persona, and if so, would she, do you think, have been spared the pathetic death of such a regression?

"In such a case could you explain how the mediatory function could be created? Is it correct to call it a creation, a new thing formed from the opposites?"

Dr. Jung: Certainly the girl would have been spared much by analysis, and her development could have been a much smoother one. The point of analysis is the making conscious of unconscious contents in order to avoid such mistakes.

As to the mediatory function, the principle can be explained very well by such a case. In order to explain it we need the principle of the opposites. The girl in question lived in a milieu that was too narrow for her gifts, and she could find in it no horizon, her environment being conspicuous for its insufficiency in ideas; it was narrow-minded and meager in every sense. Her unconscious, on the other hand, presented exactly the reverse picture. There she was surrounded by the ghosts of very important people. Such a tension as these two extremes induce is the basis of the mediatory function. She tried to live it out through her mediumistic circle and to find there the chance to come out of the impasse in which she lived. And so the tension between her real life and her unreal life increased. In reality she was,

---

[1] The transcript omits the dates of the lectures, but as it is assumed that the sixteen lectures, from 23 March to 6 July, continued to take place on each Monday, the evident date has been supplied. / Questions in quotation marks had usually been submitted to Jung in writing.

9

as I said, a little midinette; in her séances she was a person fit to associate with great minds. When such an opposition as that occurs,
something must happen to bring things together.

It is a situation that is always difficult to handle. If, for example, I
had told her she was an important person in her unconscious, I might
have started up a wrong fantasy system in her, the best way for her
to meet her problem having been to get into life and do something.
Thus I may be told that I am a big man, and told that by a thousand
people, but I can't believe it unless I can put myself to the test and
accomplish something. In her case this was difficult to achieve, for
there was always the danger that, in disentangling herself from the
false elements in the unconscious fantasies, she might also lose connection with the desirable things and thus lose belief in herself. The
analyst can never be sure that in making the patient throw away a
wrong *form*, he is not going to throw away the contained value.

For this girl, the operation of the mediatory function seems to have
followed this order: First she began speaking of ghosts, then she began to be in contact with the "ghost" of the grandfather, who had
been a sort of family god. The grandfather's way had been the right
way, and whatever came from him was exalted. Then Goethe and all
sorts of great people came into her fantasies. And finally there was
developed the important personality with which she identified herself. It was as though each of the great personages had left a deposit
in her out of which grew her greater personality. As you know, Plato
laid down the principle that it is impossible to look at something ugly
without taking something of it into the soul, and it is equally impossible to be in contact with what is beautiful without reacting to it.
Something of the sort happened to the girl.

The figure which she developed is the mediatory symbol. It is the
living form into which she slowly developed. Thus there is created an
attitude which liberates from the pairs of opposites. She detached
herself from the cheapness of her surroundings on the one hand,
and on the other from the ghosts which did not belong to her. One
could say that nature working alone works along the lines of the mediatory or transcendent function, but one has to admit that sometimes nature works against us and brings the wrong personality into
reality, so to speak. Our prisons and hospitals are full of people with
whom nature has been experimenting to unhappy ends.

Mrs. Dunham: Why did the girl revert to the condition of a child?

Dr. Jung: It was due to the fading of her libido, which contracted
more and more following prematurely the ordinary life curve which

tends always to show the maintenance of a certain tension. In youth the libido fills out a frame of generous proportions, while in old age it contracts to a much smaller amplitude.

Going back to the transcendent function, on the one side are to be found the real facts, on the other the imagination. This brings about the two poles. In the case of the girl, the ghosts went much too far on the side of imagination, and the reality side was much too small. When she put herself into reality she was a first-rate tailoress.

Fantasy is the creative function—the living form is a result of fantasy. Fantasy is a pre-stage of the symbol, but it is an essential characteristic of the symbol that it is not mere fantasy. We count upon fantasy to take us out of the impasse; for though people are not always eager to recognize the conflicts that are upsetting their lives, the dreams are always at work trying to tell on the one hand of the conflict, and on the other hand of the creative fantasy that will lead the way out. Then it becomes a matter of bringing the material into consciousness. One admits that one is in an impasse and gives free rein to the fantasy, but at the same time, the conscious must keep control in order to have a check on the tendency of nature to experiment. That is to say, one has to keep in mind that the unconscious can produce something disastrous to us. But on the other hand, one must be careful not to prescribe to the unconscious—it may be that a new way is required, and even one beset with disaster. Life often demands the trying out of new ways that are entirely unacceptable to the time in which we live, but we cannot shrink from undertaking a new way for that reason. Luther, for example, was forced into a way of life that seemed almost criminal, viewed by the standards of his time.

Dr. de Angulo's questions: (1) "When you read Schopenhauer for the first time, you rejected the viewpoint through which he has most influenced the world, namely his negation of life, and chose instead the one in which he leans toward a purposive principle in life. At the time you were making that choice, the main current of philosophic thought must have been in direct opposition to it. I would like to know more about why you made the choice that you did. Had you a leaning that way before you read Schopenhauer, or did Schopenhauer formulate that conception for you for the first time? Did your observations of the girl help you to understand Schopenhauer's argument, or did he explain the girl to you, or did it work both ways?"

(2) "It is not clear to me whether you believed that the purposive principle which you thought could be traced out in the workings of the unconscious was something that applied to the life of the individ-

ual alone, or whether it was a part of a general purposive principle that directs the universe from behind the scenes, so to speak."

(3) "I understood you to say that it is a general psychological law that the attainment of a higher level of development is always at the cost of some apparently terrible mistake. I take it for granted that the analytical experience enables one to avoid the mistake, but substitutes for it the principle of sacrifice. Is that correct?"

Dr. Jung: (1) From Schopenhauer I first got the idea of the universal urge of will, and the notion that this might be purposive. It helped me very much in working out the problem the girl presented, because I thought I could trace clearly in her signs of something working in the unconscious toward a goal.

(2) I became interested in the nature of the unconscious and asked myself if it were blind. This I could answer with no, it is generally purposive. But if one asks if the unconscious is the world or if it is psychology, then the question becomes ticklish. It was not possible for me to think of the brain as the background of the universe, and so I did not extend the purposive principle to the universe. But now I have had to modify my viewpoint with respect to the relation between the unconscious and the universe. If I think of the question purely intellectually I still say what I said before. But there is another way of looking at it—that is, we can ask, "Is there a need in us to satisfy these metaphysical problems?" How can we arrive at a suitable answer to this question? The intellect denies itself before the task. But there is another way of tackling it. Suppose, for example, we are concerned with a certain historical problem. If I had five hundred years at my disposal I could solve it. Well now, I have within myself a "man" who is millions of years old, and he perhaps can throw light on these metaphysical problems. If we put these things up to the unconscious, when we get the view that suits the "old man" things go right. If I am holding views that are out of keeping with the unconscious, they are certain to make me ill, and so it is safe for me to assume that they contradict some main current in the universe.

Does this answer suit you, Dr. de Angulo?

Dr. de Angulo: I think I understand what you mean by it, but I can't accept it.

Dr. Jung: Shall we argue it further?

Dr. de Angulo: No.

Dr. Jung: Then as to your third question, I would not go so far as to say we can avoid all mistakes by analysis, otherwise one could analyze life instead of living. One should be willing to make mistakes cheerfully. The most perfect analysis cannot prevent error. Sometimes you must go into error; moreover, the moral things in you cannot come out until you give them a chance. The recognition of truth cannot come to daylight till you have given yourself a chance to err. I believe firmly in the role that darkness and error play in life. When analysis is based on a sound technique it surely does take one not only out of night into day, but the other way around also. It is perfectly true you can substitute a sacrifice for some grotesque nonsense or other.

Dr. Mann's question: "If Nietzsche had been able or willing to make the ideal of Zarathustra real in his own life, would the book ever have been written?"

Dr. Jung: I believe the book would certainly have been written in any case, because there is a tremendous urge in a creative mind to get the product of the fantasy down in some relatively permanent form in order to hold it. Thus practically all peoples have made idols in order to give permanence and concretization to their ideals. One might say that every symbol seeks to be concretized. With this in mind, when we read in the Old Testament that it was engraved upon the stone, "Up to here God has helped us,"[2] we know that it was done in the effort to hold on to the faith that had brought them that far. Egypt had pyramids and embalming in order to concretize the principle of immortality. In the same way, Nietzsche felt the need to materialize his symbol.

That is the regular course of events. One first creates the symbol and then one says to oneself, "How does this thing happen?" or "What does it mean to me?" This, to be sure, requires a strongly reflective mind which most artists have not got, but which Nietzsche did have to a high degree. The artist in general, when he has not got the reflective mind, wants to get away from his work as soon as possible. He especially wants to get away from the image and hates to talk about it. Thus Spitteler,[3] soon after *Types* appeared, gave a lecture in which he cursed the people who want to understand symbols; the *Olympische Frühling*, according to him, has no symbolic meaning, and if you seek for one in it, it is just as if you tried to get symbolism out of the song whistled by a bird. Of course, Spitteler is loaded with symbolism; the only thing is that he does not want to see it, and in

[2] I Samuel 7:12: "And Samuel took a stone . . . and called the name of it Eben-ezer, saying, Hitherto hath the Lord helped us."

[3] Carl Spitteler (1845–1924), Swiss poet, whose epics *Prometheus and Epimetheus* (1881) and *Olympic Spring* (1900) Jung treated in *Psychological Types* (orig. 1921; CW 6).

fact the artist is often actually afraid to see it and to know what his work means. Analysis is fatal to second-rate artists, but that should be a feather in its cap. In analysis, or in an analyzed person, only something big comes through, whereas it is the tendency of our times to make it easy for every little cat or worm to be born into the art world. Everyone who uses a brush is an artist, everyone who uses a pen is a writer. Analysis puts such "artists" out of the running, it is poison to them.

Dr. Gordon: What is the person who brings forth "cats" and "worms" to think of them?

Dr. Jung: He is to think that his is a hard life when, after a day of work, he must still labor over such things. This is a burden imposed upon him by his unconscious, but he must not mix up the products thus created with art.

LECTURE

The fact that convinced me of the truth of Freud's theory was the evidence of repressions which I could find in my association experiments. Patients could not respond to certain tests where pain entered in, and when I asked why they could not respond to the stimulus word, they always said they did not know why, but when they said this it was always in a peculiar, artificial manner. I said to myself that this must be the thing that Freud described as repression. Practically all the mechanisms of repression became clear in my experiments.

As to the content of the repression, I could not agree with Freud. In those days he was speaking only of sexual trauma and shocks to explain the repression. I had had then considerable experience with cases of neurosis in which sexual things were of quite secondary importance compared with the role played by social adaptation. The case of the mediumistic girl, for example, was one such.

super ego

LECTURE 3

6 April 1925[1]

Dr. Jung:

It must not be thought that the task of getting a proper understanding of Freud, or, I should rather say, the task of getting him properly placed in my life, was an easy one for me. At that time I was planning an academic career and was about to complete a work that would advance me in the university.[2] Freud, definitely *persona non grata* in the medical world at that time, was hardly mentioned above a whisper by people of importance; at the congresses he was discussed only in the *couloirs*, never on the floor, and any connection with him was a menace to one's own reputation. Therefore the discovery by me that my experiments in association were directly connected with Freud's theories was most unwelcome. One time while I was in my laboratory, it flashed into my mind that Freud had actually elaborated a theory which would explain my experiments. At the same time a devil whispered in my ear that I could perfectly well publish my work without mentioning Freud, that I had worked out my experiments long before I knew of Freud, and so could claim complete independence of him as far as they went. However, I saw at once that there was an element of lying involved which I did not propose to go in for. So I openly took up the cudgels for Freud and fought for him in the subsequent congresses. There came a certain lecturer to one of these, and gave an explanation of the neuroses entirely ignoring Freud. I protested at this, and engaged in my first fight for Freud's ideas. Later on, at another congress, there was a lecture on the compulsion neuroses, and again mention of Freud's

[1] Parts of the contents of this lecture appear, considerably revised, in chapters IV and V of *MDR*.

[2] Cf. *MDR*, pp. 147ff./145ff. Jung became a privatdocent in Zurich University in 1905 (ibid., 117/118).

work was omitted.[3] This time I wrote an article in a well-known German newspaper, attacking the man. Immediately a flood of resistances was released against me, and that man wrote me a letter and warned me that my academic future was at stake if I persisted in joining forces with Freud. Of course I felt that if I had to get an academic future at such a price, it could be damned, and I went on writing about Freud.

All this while I continued my experiments, but still could not get myself into agreement with Freud as to the origin of all neuroses being sex-repression. Freud had published thirteen cases of hysteria,[4] all of which were reported as the result of sexual violation. Later, when I met Freud, he said that about some of these cases, at least, he had been fooled. One of them, for instance, was of a girl who said that when she was four years old she had been violated by her father. This man happened to be a friend of Freud's, and the latter convinced himself that the girl's story was a lie. Subsequent investigation brought out the fact that others in the series were also falsifications, but he would not retract, it having been his policy always to let things stand as he originally presented them. There is then a certain untrustworthiness about all these earlier cases. Thus again, the famous first case that he had with Breuer,[5] which has been so much spoken about as an example of a brilliant therapeutic success, was in reality nothing of the kind. Freud told me that he was called in to see the woman the same night that Breuer had seen her for the last time,[6] and that she was in a bad hysterical attack, due to the breaking off of the transference. This, then, was no cure at all in the sense in which it was originally presented, and yet it was a very interesting case, so interesting that there was no need to claim for it something that did not happen. But all of these things I did not know at that time.

[3] The lecturers were Gustav Aschaffenburg and/or Alfred E. Hoche, at congresses at Baden-Baden and Tübingen in 1906 and at Amsterdam in 1907. See *Freud/Jung*, 2 J (5 Oct. 1906), 6 J (26 Nov. 1906), and 43–44 J (4 and 11 Sept. 1907); and Jung's first two papers in CW 4. Jung's recollections in this seminar, which of course were spoken off the cuff, sometimes diverge from what is recorded in the *Letters* and other documents.

[4] In *Studies on Hysteria* (1893; SE II) there are four case histories by Freud; Appendix B, a list of writings by Freud on conversion hysteria, cites eleven other publications before 1906.

[5] For Josef Breuer's case history of Anna O., see SE II, pp. 21–47. Jung cited the *Studies on Hysteria* as early as 1902; see CW 1, n. 114.

[6] Freud's professional call on Anna O. at this time is not mentioned in the literature. Cf. Peter Gay, *Freud: A Life for Our Time* (New York and London, 1988), pp. 66–67.

Besides my experiments, I was working with many cases of insanity, particularly with dementia praecox.[7] At that time there was no psychological viewpoint to be found in the field of psychiatry. A label was put on each case; it was said to be a degeneration here, or an atrophy there, and then it was finished—there was nothing more to be done about it. It was only among the nurses that any psychological interest in the patients could be found, and among them there were some very shrewd guesses offered as to the conditions presented; but the doctors knew none of this.

For example, there was an old case in the women's ward,[8] a woman who was seventy-five years old, and who had lain in bed for forty years. She had been in the asylum nearly fifty years perhaps—so long, in fact, that no one remembered her entrance because the people there at the time were all dead. There was just one head nurse, who had been in the asylum thirty-five years, who knew something of this woman's early history. This old patient could not talk, and could only eat liquid food which she took with her fingers with a peculiar shovelling movement, so that it sometimes took her two hours to get down a cup of food. When she was not feeding herself, she was making most peculiar movements with her hands and arms. I thought to myself as I looked at her, "What a terrible thing is this." But that is as far as I got with it. She was regularly presented in clinic as an old case of dementia praecox, catatonic form. It seemed to me perfect nonsense to dispose of these extraordinary movements in that way.

This case and its effect on me were typical of my whole reaction to psychiatry. For six months I was struggling desperately to find myself in it, and was all the time more and more baffled. I was deeply humiliated to see that my chief[9] and my colleagues seemed to feel sure of themselves, and that it was only I who was drifting helplessly. My failure to understand gave me such feelings of inferiority that I could not bear to go out of the hospital. Here was I, a man with a profession which I could not rightly grasp. I therefore stayed in all the time and gave myself up to the study of my cases.

Late one evening, as I went through the ward and saw the old woman I have described, I asked myself, "Why should that be?" I went to the head nurse and asked if it had always been that way with that patient. "Yes," she said, "but formerly I heard from the head of

[7] "The Psychology of Dementia Praecox" (1907), CW 3, pars. 1ff.
[8] "The Content of the Psychoses" (1908), CW 3, par. 358. Cf. MDR, pp. 124ff./125ff.
[9] Paul Eugen Bleuler (1857–1939), director of the Burghölzli Hospital 1898–1927.

the men's ward that she used to make shoes!" I looked up the archives and mention was made of the fact that she made movements
as if making shoes. Early shoemakers held the shoe between their
knees and pulled the thread through with movements exactly like the
ones the old woman used to make. One can still see them doing it in
certain primitive places.

Some time after this the patient died. Then her brother three years
older than herself turned up. "Why did your sister go insane?" I
asked him. He told me she had been in love with a shoemaker, but
for some reason the man did not want to marry her, and that she had
gone insane. She had kept alive the vision of him with those movements.

This was my first inkling of the psychogenesis of dementia praecox.
Then I kept careful watch over the cases and noted the psychogenetic
factors. It became clear to me that Freud's conceptions could throw
light on these problems. This is the origin of *The Psychology of Dementia Praecox*. I did not meet with much sympathy for my ideas. In fact,
my colleagues laughed at me. It was another example of the difficulty
felt by certain people when asked to consider a new idea.

In 1906 I worked out very carefully a case of dementia praecox.[10]
Again it was a dress-maker, but this time not a young girl, but an old
one of fifty-six and so ugly that when Freud came to visit the hospital,
and asked to see the patient I had worked on, he was thunderstruck,
and marveled that I could stand working with so ugly a human being.
But this patient made a great impression on me.

She came from the old part of Zurich where the streets are narrow
and dirty, and where she not only was born in misery, but grew up in
it likewise. Her sister was a prostitute, her father a drinker. She went
insane with the paranoid form of dementia praecox, that is to say,
she had ideas of grandeur mixed with ideas of suppression, or of
inferiority as we would say now. I took down her material in great
detail, and often while we were talking her voices would interrupt,
saying something like this: "Tell the doctor that all you are saying is
bunk, and that he need pay no attention to it." Or sometimes when
she would be protesting violently at being kept in the asylum, the
voices would say, "You know perfectly well you are insane and belong
right where you are." Naturally she had great resistances to the

---

[10] That of B. St., or Babette S., principal case in "The Psychology of Dementia Praecox," pars. 198ff.; also in "The Content of the Psychoses" (1908), CW 3, pars. 363ff.
Cf. *MDR*, pp. 125–28 (both eds.).

voices. I got the idea that the unconscious was entirely on top, and that her ego-consciousness had gone into the unconscious. I discovered further, to my astonishment and bewilderment, that the ideas of megalomania and those of depreciation came of one and the same source. The ideas of depreciation were those of being ill-treated or wronged or of being bad. These I called self-depreciation, while the ideas of megalomania I called self-appreciation. At the beginning I held it for impossible that the unconscious could produce the opposites together in this way for I was still on the Schopenhauer-Hartmann-Freud trail. The unconscious was only an urge and could not display a conflict within itself. Then I thought perhaps the two came from different levels of the unconscious, but that would not work; and finally I had to admit that the woman's mind was using both principles at once.

[margin note: The principle of opposites]

Later cases corroborated my findings. For example, I had the case of a very intelligent lawyer who was suffering from paranoia. In these cases there is just one idea about which they are insane, namely persecution; otherwise they are adapted to reality. The case develops somewhat as follows: A man thinks he notices people talking about him; then he asks himself why, and answers it by saying that he must be someone important whom other people want to crush. Little by little he finds he is a Messiah who must be annihilated. The man of whom I am speaking was dangerous in that he had attempted one murder, and when he was free attempted another. He had held an important political position, and one could talk to him. He hated the doctors and spent his time cursing them. Once he broke down with me and said, "I know that alienists are the very finest people." Then he fainted. This moment came after I had worked with him three hours. When he came to again, he was in his old state of depreciation. The depreciation is produced as compensation to the megalomania. I insist on this point so much because it is back of the Yea and Nay in the unconscious; in other words, the unconscious contains the pairs of opposites.

Through this book on dementia praecox I came to Freud.[11] We met in 1906. The first day I met him it was at one o'clock in the afternoon, and we talked steadily for thirteen hours. He was the first man of real importance I had seen; no one else could compare with

[11] Cf. *MDR*, p. 149/146: "through this book I came to know Freud." Jung sent Freud a copy of *Über die Psychologie der Dementia praecox* (1907) in December 1906: *Freud/Jung*, 9 J. Jung and his wife first visited the Freuds, in Vienna, on March 3, 1907: ibid., p. 24.

him. I found him extremely shrewd, intelligent, and altogether remarkable. But my first impressions of him were somewhat confused;
I could not quite make him out. I found him, though, absolutely serious about his sex theory, and in his attitude there was nothing trivial to be found. It made a great impression on me, but still I had
grave doubts. I told him this, and whenever I did, he always said it
was because I had not had enough experience. It was a fact that in
those days I had not had enough experience upon which to form a
critique. I could see that this sexual theory was enormously important
to Freud, both personally and philosophically, but I could not make
out whether it came from a personal bias or not, so I went away with
a doubt in my mind about the whole situation.

Another impression I got in connection with this seriousness of
Freud with respect to his theory of sexuality was this: He invariably
sneered at spirituality as being nothing but repressed sexuality, and
so I said if one were committed fully to the logic of that position, then
one must say that our whole civilization is farcical, nothing but a morbid creation due to repressed sexuality. He said, "Yes, so it is, and its
being so is just a curse of fate we cannot help."[12] My mind was quite
unwilling to settle there, but still I could not argue it out with him.

A third impression of those days involves things that became clear
to me only much later, things that I thought out fully only after our
friendship was gone. When Freud talked of sexuality it was as though
he were talking of God—as a man would talk who had undergone a
conversion. It was like the Indians talking of the sun with tears in
their eyes. I remember one Indian coming up softly behind me while
I was looking at the mountain over the pueblo, and saying quite suddenly in my ear, "Don't you think all life is coming from the mountain?"[13] It was just in that way that Freud talked of sexuality. A peculiar emotional quality would come into his face, and the cause of it
I was at a loss to understand. Finally I seemed to make it out through
the consideration of something else that remained obscure to me
then, namely Freud's bitterness. One might say Freud consists of bitterness, every word being loaded with it. His attitude was the bitterness of the person who is entirely misunderstood, and his manner
always seemed to say, "If they don't understand they must be
stamped into Hell." I noticed this in him the first time I met him, and

[12] Cf. *MDR*, p. 150/147.

[13] Jung had visited the Taos Pueblo, in New Mexico, three months earlier, for a day
or two during January 1925. Cf. *MDR*, p. 252/237, and William McGuire, "Jung in
America, 1924–1925," *Spring*, 1978, pp. 37–53.

always saw it in him, but I could not find the connection with his attitude toward sexuality.

The explanation seems to me to be this: Freud, for all his repudiation of spirituality, has in reality a mystical attitude toward sexuality. When one protested to him that a certain poem could not be understood on a sexual basis exclusively, he would say, "No, certainly not, that is psychosexuality." But when analyzing the poem, he would pull out this thread and that, and so on until nothing was left but sexuality. Now I think sexuality is a double concept to him, on the one side the mystical element, on the other mere sexuality, but the latter is the only thing that comes out in his terminology because he will not admit he has the other side. That he has the other side, I think, is obvious from the way he showed his emotions. And so he is forever defeating his own purpose. He wants to teach that sexuality contains spirituality looked at from within, but he uses only concretistic sex terminology and conveys just the wrong idea. His bitterness comes from this fact of constantly working against himself, for there is no bitterness worse than that of a man who is his own worst enemy.

Freud is blind to the dualism of the unconscious. He does not know that the thing that wells up has an inside and an outside, and that if you talk only of the latter you speak of the shell alone. But there is nothing to be done about this conflict in him; the only chance would be if he could have an experience that would make him see spirituality working inside the shell. However, his intellect would then inevitably strip it to "mere" sexuality. I tried to present to him cases showing other factors than sexual ones but always he would have it that there was nothing there save repressed sexuality.

As I said, such terribly bitter people are always those who work against themselves. When I work against myself I project the uncertainty and terror that I feel. If I am to avoid this, the one thing to settle is myself. Freud does not know that the unconscious produces a factor to counteract the monistic principle to which he has given himself over. I find him a tragic figure, for he is a great man, but it is a fact that he runs away from himself. He never asks himself why he has to talk about sex all the time, and in this running away from himself he is like any other artist. In fact, creative people are usually like that.

These thoughts came to me, as I said, chiefly after I had broken with Freud. I give them to you because as you know, my relation to Freud has long since become a matter of public discussion, and so I must present my view of it.

I came away from my first visit to Freud feeling that the sexual factor must be taken most seriously. Somewhat bewildered, I began to look at my cases again and kept pretty quiet. In 1909 Freud and I were both invited to Clark University, and we were together daily for about seven weeks.[14] We analyzed dreams each day, and it was then that I got an impression, a fatal one, of his limitations. I had two dreams out of which he could not make head or tail. Of course I did not mind that, for the very greatest person is going to have that experience with dreams some time or other. It was just a human limitation, and I would never have taken it as a reason for not going on; on the contrary, I wanted very much to go on—I felt myself to be his son. Then something happened which put a stop to it.

Freud had a dream on an important theme which I cannot mention. I analyzed it and said there was more to be said if he would give me some points about his private life. He looked at me with a peculiar expression of suspicion in his eyes and said, "I could tell you more but I can't risk my authority." Then I knew further analysis was impossible because he put authority above truth. I said I would have to stop there, and I never asked him again for material. You must understand that I speak here quite objectively, but I must include this experience with Freud, because it is the most important factor in my relation to him. He could not bear any criticism whatsoever.

As Freud could only partially handle my dreams, the amount of symbolical material in them increased as it always does until it is understood. If one remains with a narrow point of view about the dream material, there comes a feeling of dissociation and one feels blind and deaf. When this happens to an isolated man he petrifies.

On my way back from America, I had a dream that was the origin of my book on the *Psychology of the Unconscious*.[15] In those times I had no idea of the collective unconscious; I thought of the conscious as of a room above, with the unconscious as a cellar underneath and then the earth wellspring, that is, the body, sending up the instincts. These

---

[14] Cf. *MDR*, pp. 156, 158/152, 154.

[15] Jung published *Wandlungen und Symbole der Libido: Beiträge zur Entwicklungsgeschichte des Denkens* originally as two parts, in the *Jahrbuch für psychoanalytische und psychopathologische Forschungen*, 1911 and 1912, and in book form 1912; tr. Beatrice M. Hinkle, with the title *Psychology of the Unconscious: A Study of the Transformations and Symbolisms of the Libido; A Contribution to the History of the Evolution of Thought*, 1916. Comprehensively revised and expanded as *Symbole der Wandlung: Analyse des Vorspiels zu einer Schizophrenie*. 1952; tr., *Symbols of Transformation: An Analysis of the Prelude to a Case of Schizophrenia*, 1956 (CW 5). / In *MDR*, p. 158/154, Jung called the dream "a kind of prelude to my book."

instincts tend to disagree with our conscious ideals and so we keep them down. That is the figure I had always used for myself, and then came this dream which I hope I can tell without being too personal.

I dreamed I was in a medieval house, a big, complicated house with many rooms, passages, and stairways. I came in from the street and went down into a vaulted Gothic room, and from there into a cellar. I thought to myself that now I was at the bottom, but then I found a square hole. With a lantern in my hand I peeped down this hole, and saw stairs leading further down, and down these I climbed. They were dusty stairs, very much worn, and the air was sticky, the whole atmosphere very uncanny. I came to another cellar, this one of very ancient structure, perhaps Roman, and again there was a hole through which I could look down into a tomb filled with prehistoric pottery, bones, and skulls; as the dust was undisturbed, I thought I had made a great discovery. There I woke up.

Freud said this dream meant that there were certain people associated with me whom I wanted dead, and buried under two cellars, but I thought the meaning was entirely elsewhere though I could not make it out. I kept thinking this way: The cellar is the unconscious, but what is the medieval house? This I did not make out until much later. But there was something below both cellars even—that is, remains of prehistoric man. What does that mean? I had a strongly impersonal feeling about the dream. Involuntarily I began to make fantasies about it, though I did not then know anything about the principle of fantasizing in order to bring up unconscious material. I said to myself, "Isn't it fine to make excavations. Where am I going to have a chance to do that?" And actually when I came home I looked up a place where excavations were being made, and went to it.

But of course that did not satisfy me. My thoughts then beginning to turn to the East, I began to read about excavations being made in Babylonia.[16] My interest went to books, and I came upon a German book called *Mythology and Symbolism*. I went through the three or four volumes at top speed, reading like mad, in fact, until I became as bewildered as ever I had been in the clinic. I had left the hospital, by the way, in 1909,[17] after being there eight years, but now it seemed to me I was living in an insane asylum of my own making. I went

[16] That is, Mesopotamia. / The work Jung turned to was Friedrich Creuzer, *Symbolik und Mythologie der alten Völker* (Leipzig and Darmstadt, 1810–1823). Cf. *MDR*, p. 162/158.

[17] *Freud/Jung*, 140 J, 12 May 1909; *MDR*, p. 117/119.

about with all these fantastic figures: centaurs, nymphs, satyrs, gods and goddesses, as though they were patients and I was analyzing them. I read a Greek or a Negro myth as if a lunatic were telling me his anamnesis—I lost myself in puzzling what it could possibly mean.

Slowly out of all this came the *Psychology of the Unconscious*, for in the midst of it I came upon the Miller fantasies,[18] and they acted like a catalyser upon all the material I had gathered together in my mind. I saw in Miss Miller a person who, like myself, had had mythological fantasies, fantasies and dreams of a thoroughly impersonal character. Their impersonality I readily recognized, as well as the fact that they must come from the lower "cellars," though I did not give the name of collective unconscious to them. This then is the way the book grew up.

While working on the book I was haunted by bad dreams. I feel that I must speak of my dreams even though one is unavoidably personal to a degree when one does so. But dreams have influenced all the important changes in my life and theories. Thus for example I came to study medicine by reason of a dream, it having been my firm intention at first to become an archeologist. With this in view I had entered my name in the list of students of philosophy at the University, but then came this dream, and I changed everything.[19] At that time, I mean when I was working on the *Psychology of the Unconscious*, all my dreams pointed to a break with Freud. I thought, of course, that he would accept the cellars below his cellar, but the dreams were preparing me for the contrary. Freud could see nothing in the book but resistance to the father,[20] and the point in it to which he took the greatest exception was my contention that the libido is split and produces the thing that checks itself. This to him as a monist was utter blasphemy. From this attitude of Freud's I felt more than ever con-

[18] (Miss) Frank Miller, an American student at the University of Geneva, wrote a memoir describing her fantasies, "Some Instances of Subconscious Creative Imagination," published (in French) in *Archives de psychologie* (Geneva, vol. V, 1906), with an introduction by the psychologist Théodore Flournoy, who was treating her. See below, Lecture 4, n. 1.

[19] Dream about a radiolarian: *MDR*, p. 85/90f. Illustrated in *Jung: Word and Image*, p. 90.

[20] A story is current that Freud returned Jung's book with the inscription "Resistance against the father!" But a copy of the first edition is in Freud's library in London, inscribed by Jung "Laid at the feet of the Teacher and Master by his disobedient but grateful pupil." (*Freud/Jung*, new ed., 324F n. 2, addendum.) Also see *Jung: Letters*, vol. 1, p. 73, in a letter of March 4, 1930: "Freud had accepted my copy, but he told me that my whole idea meant nothing but resistances against the father."

vinced that his idea of God was placed in sexuality, and that libido is to him only an urge in one direction. As a matter of fact, however, I think it can be shown that there is a will to die as well as a will to live. We prepare ourselves for death when we reach the summit of life; or, to put it in another way, after the age of thirty-five, let us say, we begin to know that cooler winds are blowing—at first we don't understand, but later we cannot escape the meaning.

After this break I had with Freud, the pupils that I had all over the world left me and turned to Freud.[21] They were told that my book was rubbish, and that I was a mystic, and with that the matter was settled. Suddenly I found myself completely isolated. This, however disadvantageous it may have been, had also an advantage for me as an introvert; that is it encouraged the vertical movement of the libido. Cut off from the horizontal movement which activity in the outside world brings, I was driven to investigate fully the things within myself.

When I finished the *Psychology of the Unconscious*, I had a peculiarly lucid moment in which I surveyed my path as far as I had come. I thought: "Now you have the key to mythology and you have the power to unlock all doors." But then something within me said: "Why unlock all these doors?"[22] And then I found myself asking what I had done after all. I had written a book about the hero, I had explained the myths of past peoples, but what about my own myth? I had to admit I had none; I knew theirs but none of my own, nor did anyone else have one today. Moreover, we were without an understanding of the unconscious. Around these reflections, as around a central core, grew all the ideas that came to partial expression in the book on types.

[21] Cf. *MDR*, pp. 167f./162: "[Franz] Riklin and [Alphonse] Maeder alone stuck by me." Others who remained with Jung included J. B. Lang, Mary Moltzer, Antonia Wolff, Hans Schmid-Guisan, Martha Böddinghaus (Sigg), J. Vodoz, C. Schneiter, Adolf Keller, Jan Nelken, Beatrice M. Hinkle, and (for a time) Smith Ely Jelliffe and Trigant Burrow.

[22] Cf. *MDR*, p. 171/165.

LECTURE 4

13 April 1925

Dr. Mann's question: "Is it not by intuition that one arrives most easily at the transcendent function, and if a person is lacking in that function—that is, in intuition—are not the difficulties greatly increased? Must one not reach the transcendent function alone, that is, unaided?"

Dr. Jung: It depends very much on the person's type as to what part intuition plays in finding the transcendent function. If the superior function is intuition, for example, then the intuitions are directly in the way, since the transcendent function is made, or takes place, between the superior and the inferior functions. The inferior function can only come up at the expense of the superior, so that in the intuitive type the intuitions have to be overcome, so to speak, in order for the transcendent function to be found. On the other hand, if the person is a sensation type, then the intuitions are the inferior function, and the transcendent function may be said to be arrived at through intuition. It is a fact that in analysis it often seems as though intuition were the most important of the functions, but that is only so because analysis is a laboratory experiment and not reality.

LECTURE

At our last meeting I told you all that I could about the making of the *Psychology of the Unconscious* and its effect on me. It was published in 1912, as *Wandlungen und Symbole der Libido*. The problem it brought to focus in my mind was that of the hero myth in relation to our own times. With the fundamental thesis of the book, namely the splitting of the libido into a positive and a negative current, Freud

26

was, as I have said, in utter disagreement. The publishing of the book marks the end of our friendship.

Today I would like to speak about the subjective aspect of the *Psychology of the Unconscious*. When one writes such a book, one has the idea that one is writing about certain objective material, and in my case I thought I was merely handling the Miller fantasies with a certain point in view together with the attendant mythological material. It took me a long time to see that a painter could paint a picture and think the matter ended there and had nothing whatever to do with himself. And in the same way it took me several years to see that it, the *Psychology of the Unconscious*, can be taken as myself and that an analysis of it leads inevitably into an analysis of my own unconscious processes. Difficult as it is to do this in a lecture, it is this aspect I would like to discuss, tracing out especially the ways in which the book seemed to forecast the future.

As you remember, the book begins with a statement about two kinds of thinking that can be observed: intellectual or directed thinking, and fantastic or passive automatic thinking. In the process of directed thinking, thoughts are handled as tools, they are made to serve the purposes of the thinker; while in passive thinking thoughts are like individuals going about on their own as it were. Fantastical thinking knows no hierarchy; the thoughts may even be antagonistic to the ego.

I took Miss Miller's fantasies as such an autonomous form of thinking, but I did not realize that she stood for that form of thinking in myself. She took over my fantasy and became stage director to it, if one interprets the book subjectively. In other words, she became an anima figure, a carrier of an inferior function of which I was very little conscious. I was in my consciousness an active thinker accustomed to subjecting my thoughts to the most rigorous sort of direction, and therefore fantasizing was a mental process that was directly repellent to me. As a form of thinking I held it to be altogether impure, a sort of incestuous intercourse, thoroughly immoral from an intellectual viewpoint. Permitting fantasy in myself had the same effect on me as would be produced on a man if he came into his workshop and found all the tools flying about doing things independently of his will. It shocked me, in other words, to think of the possibility of a fantasy life in my own mind; it was against all the intellectual ideals I had developed for myself, and so great was my resistance to it, that I could only admit the fact in myself through the process of projecting my material into Miss Miller's. Or, to put it even more strongly, passive thinking seemed to me such a weak and perverted thing that I could only handle it through a diseased woman. As a matter of fact, Miss Miller did afterwards become entirely deranged. During the war I had a letter from the man who was Miss Miller's doctor in America, telling me that my analysis of her fantasy material had been a perfectly correct one, that in her insanity the cosmogonic myths touched upon had come fully to light. Also Flournoy, who had her under observation at the time I first read her material, told me that my analysis had been correct.[1] There was such a tremendous activity of the collective unconscious that it is not surprising she was finally overcome.

I had to realize then that in Miss Miller I was analyzing my own fantasy function, which because it was so repressed, like hers, was semi-morbid. When a function is repressed that way, it becomes contaminated by material from the collective unconscious. So Miss Miller would, in a way, be a description of my impure thinking; and thus in this book the question of the inferior function and the anima comes up.

In the second part of the book there comes the "Hymn of Creation."[2] This is the positive expression of the unfolding of energy: or generating power—it is the way up. The "Song of the Moth"[3] is the way down; it is light created, and then creating going to its end, a kind of enantiodromia. In the first case it is the period of growth, of youth, of light and summer. In the moth the libido is shown to burn its wings in the light it has created before; it is going to kill itself in the same urge that brought it to birth. With this duality in the cosmic principle, the book ends. It leads up to the pairs of opposites, that is, to the beginning of the *Types*.[4]

The next portion of the book deals with creative energy in a differ-

---

[1] CW 5, p. xxviii: Foreword to the Second (German) Edition [of *Wandlungen und Symbole der Libido*] (November, 1924). This foreword was not included in later editions of *Psychology of the Unconscious*; it first appeared in English in CW 5 (1956).

[2] CW 5, pars. 46ff.: chapter IV of part one (not the second part of the book). Miller fantasized a "dream poem" entitled "Glory to God," which upon waking she wrote in an album. (Cf. S. T. Coleridge, "Kublai Khan.")

[3] Ibid., pars. 115ff.: chapter V. Miller similarly produced a poem she entitled "The Moth to the Sun."

[4] *Psychologische Typen* (1921); tr. H. G. Baynes, *Psychological Types* (1923), with the added subtitle "The Psychology of Individuation," which was not carried over into subsequent editions, either English (CW 6) or German. The CW and GW editions include an appendix containing four related papers (see below, n. 11). Cf. *MDR*, pp. 207f./ 198f.

ent aspect. Energy can show itself in manifold forms and in a process of transition from[5] one form to another. The basic transformation is that which ensues when the energy passes from strictly biological needs into cultural achievements. From this point on it is a matter of evolution. How is it possible then to get across from the sexual, for example, to the spiritual, not only from the scientific standpoint, but as a phenomenon in the individual? Sexuality and spirituality are pairs of opposites that need each other. How is the process that leads from the sexual stage to the spiritual stage brought about?

The first image that comes up is the hero. It is a most ideal image whose qualities change from age to age, but it has always embodied the things people value the most. The hero embodies the transition we are seeking to trace, for it is as though in the sexual stage man feels too much under the power of nature, a power which he is in no way able to manage. The hero is a very perfect man, he stands out as a human protest against nature, who is seeking to rob man of that possibility of perfection. The unconscious makes the hero symbol, and therefore the hero means a change of attitude. But this hero symbol comes also from the unconscious, which is also nature, that same nature which is not the least interested in the ideal that man is struggling to formulate. Man comes then into conflict with the unconscious, and this struggle is that of winning free from his unconscious, his mother. His unconscious, as I said, forms images of perfect people, but when he tries to realize these hero types, another trend in the unconscious is aroused, [a trend] to the attempt to destroy the image. So is developed the terrible mother, the devouring dragon, the dangers of rebirth, etc. At the same time the appearance of the hero ideal means the strengthening of the hopes of man. It gives man the notion that he can reorganize the lines of his life if the mother will allow it. This can't be done by a literal rebirth, so it is accomplished by a transformation process, or psychological rebirth. But this is not to be done without serious battle with the mother. The paramount question becomes, Will the mother allow the hero to be born? And then, What can be done to satisfy the mother so that she will allow it?

Thus we come to the idea of the sacrifice as embodied in the bull-sacrifice of Mithras.[6] This is not a Christian but a Mithraic idea. The hero himself is not sacrificed, but his animal side, the bull.

[5] *Transcript*: "transifrom." Typing error?

[6] *Transcript*: "Mithra." That spelling is usual in German; "Mithras" has been adopted

A discussion of the role of the mother or unconscious as both birth-place and source of destruction leads to the idea of the dual mother role, or the existence of the pairs of opposites in the unconscious, the principle of construction and the principle of destruction. A sacrifice must be done in order to cut the hero away from the power of the unconscious and give him his individual autonomy. He has to pay himself off and contrive to fill the vacuum left in the unconscious. What is to be sacrificed? According to mythology, it is childhood, the veil of Maya, past ideals.

In connection with this I may say there is a passage in the *Psychology of the Unconscious* upon which I have often been attacked.[7] I have said there that the greatest help in getting one over the dangers of the rebirth and breaking away from the mother was to be found in regular work. Sometimes in thinking over this I have thought that was a cheap and inadequate way of meeting this tremendous problem, and then I have been inclined to side with my critics. But the more I have thought of it, the more I have been convinced that after all I was in the first place correct, and our regularly repeated efforts to throw off unconsciousness—that is, by regular work—has made our humanity. We can conquer unconsciousness by regular work but never by a grand gesture. If I say to a Negro, how do you deal with your unconscious? He gives as answer, "By work." "But," I say, "your life is all play." This he vehemently denies and explains to me that much of his life passes in the performance of the most laborious dances for the spirits. Dancing to us is really play, it is lightness and grace, but for primitives it is really hard work. All ceremonies may be said to be work, and our sense of work to be derivative therefrom.

Following this theme further, I can give the illustration of the action of the Australian Negro when he is sick. He goes to a place where his *churinga*[8] is hidden in the rocks. He rubs it. The *churinga* is full of healthy magic, and when he rubs it, this gets into his system and his sickness goes into the *churinga* which then is put back in its

in the CW. / Mithraism, which Jung used as a paradigm, was a religion widespread in the Roman Empire, ca. the 2nd cent. A.D., based on the opposition between good and evil.

[7] In the 1916 ed., p. 455 (1919 ed., p. 252.). In *Symbols of Transformation* the passage has been deleted; cf. pars. 644–45.

[8] A "soul stone" or fetish. Cf. "On Psychic Energy" (1928; CW 8), par. 119. Jung had begun that paper in 1912, soon after finishing *Wandlungen und Symbole*, but put it aside to work on the type problem ("On Psychic Energy," par. 1, n. 1). His source for the Australian aborigines was W. R. Spencer and F. J. Gillen, *The Northern Tribes of Central Australia* (1904), cited in *Psychological Types* (CW 6), especially par. 496.

place in the rocks where it can digest the sickness and refill itself with healthy magic. That replaces prayer. We would say one got strength from God through prayer, but the primitive gets strength from God by work.

If you have followed these explanations at all, you will have seen that the material could not fail to make a great impression on me, I mean the mythological material with which I was working. One of the most important influences was that I elaborated Miss Miller's morbidity into myths in a way satisfactory to myself, and so I assimilated the Miller side of myself, which did me much good. To speak figuratively, I found a lump of clay, turned it to gold and put it in my pocket. I got Miller into myself and strengthened my fantasy power by the mythological material. Then I continued my active thinking, but with hesitancy. It seemed as if my fantasy were going away from the material.

At this time I wrote little. Through the fact that I worried about my difficulty with Freud, I came to study Adler[9] carefully in order to see what was his case against Freud. I was struck at once by the difference in type.[10] Both were treating neurosis and hysteria, and yet to the one man it looked so, and to the other it was something quite different. I could find no solution. Then it dawned on me that possibly I was dealing with two different types, who were fated to approach the same set of facts from widely differing aspects. I began to see among my patients some who fit Adler's theories, and others who fit Freud's, and thus I came to formulate the theory of extraversion and introversion. There followed much discussion here and there among friends and acquaintances, through which I found that I had the tendency to project my inferior extraverted side into my extraverted friends, and they their introverted sides into me. By discussion with my personal friends, I found that because of this continued projection into them of my inferior function, I was always in danger of depreciating them. My patients I could take impersonally and objectively, but my friends I had to meet on a feeling basis, and as feeling is a relatively undifferentiated function in me, and therefore in the unconscious, it naturally carried a heavy load of projections. Little by

---

9 After Alfred Adler broke with Freud, in the spring of 1911, Jung's references to him (in his letters to Freud) were consistently negative. In autumn 1912, however, in a foreword to "The Theory of Psychoanalysis" (CW 4, p. 87), Jung wrote, "I recognize that [Adler] and I have reached similar conclusions on various points." Cf. *Freud/Jung*, 333 J, n. 1.

10 Cf. CW 6, pars. 88–92.

little I made a discovery that was shocking to me, namely the fact of this extraverted personality, which every introvert carries within him in his unconscious, and which I had been projecting upon my friends to their detriment. It was equally annoying to my extravert friends to have to admit an inferior introvert within themselves. Out of these experiences that were partly personal, I wrote a little pamphlet on the psychological types, and afterwards read it as a paper before a congress.[11] There were contained in this several mistakes which I afterwards could rectify. Thus, for example, I thought that an extravert must always be a feeling type, which was clearly a projection growing out of the fact of my own extraversion being associated with my unconscious feeling.

All of this is the outside picture of the development of my book on the types. I could perfectly well say this is the way the book came about and make an end of it there. But there is another side, a weaving about among mistakes, impure thinking, etc., etc., which is always very difficult for a man to make public. He likes to give you the finished product of his directed thinking and have you understand that so it was born in his mind, free of weakness. A thinking man's attitude toward his intellectual life is quite comparable to that of a woman toward her erotic life. If I ask a woman about the man she has married, "How did this come about?" she will say, "I met him and loved him, and that is all." She will conceal most carefully all the little back alleys of the erotic highway she has travelled, all the little meannesses, and squinting situations that she may have been involved in, and she will present you with an unrivalled perfection of smoothness. Above all she will conceal from you the erotic mistakes she has made. She will not have it that she has been weak in this her strongest function.

Just so with a man about his books. He does not want to tell of the secret alliances, the *faux pas* of his mind. This it is that makes lies of most autobiographies. Just as sexuality is in women largely unconscious, so is this inferior side of his thinking largely unconscious in a man. And just as a woman erects her stronghold of power in her sexuality, and will not give away any of the secrets of its weak side, so a man centers his power in his thinking and proposes to hold it as a solid front against the public, particularly against other men. He

[11] "A Contribution to the Study of Psychological Types" (CW 6, appendix), a lecture to the Psychoanalytic Congress in Munich, 1913 (the last time Jung and Freud met). In pars. 880–82, Jung contrasts Freud's and Adler's theories in terms of type.

thinks if he tells the truth in this field it is equivalent to turning over the keys of his citadel to the enemy.

But this other side of his thinking is not repellent to a woman, and therefore a man can usually speak freely of it to a woman, particularly to a certain sort of woman. As you know I think of women as belonging in general to two types, the mother and the hetaira.[12] The hetaira type acts as the mother for the other side of men's thinking. The very fact of its being a weak and helpless sort of thinking appeals to this sort of woman; she thinks of it as something embryonic which she helps to develop. Paradoxical as it may seem, even a cocotte may sometimes know more about the spiritual growth of a man than his own wife.

Now at this time, inasmuch as I was actively thinking, I had to find some way to reserve myself, so to speak, and to pick up the other, the passive side of my mental life. This, as I have said, a man dislikes to do because he feels so helpless. He can't quite manage it, and feels inferior—it is as though he were a log being tossed about in a stream, and so he gets out of it as soon as possible. He repudiates it because it is not pure intellect—even worse than that, it might be feeling. He feels himself a victim of all of that, and yet he must deliver himself over to it in order to get at his creative power. Since my anima had been definitely awakened by all that mythological material I had been working with, I was forced now to give attention to that other side, to my unconscious inferior side in other words. This sounds very easy I know, but it is a statement a man hates to make.

What I did then in order to get at this inferior, unconscious side of me was to make at night an exact reversal of the mental machinery I had used in the day. That is to say, I turned all my libido within in order to observe the dreams that were going on. It has been said by Léon Daudet[13] that dreams do not only appear in the sleep but, having a life of their own, they continue also during the daytime below the level of consciousness. This is of course not a new idea, but one that cannot be emphasized too often. One is able to catch dreams best

[12] Jung briefly discussed these female types in a 1927 essay; cf. "Mind and Earth," CW 10, pars. 75f. In a 1934 lecture at the Psychological Club, Zurich, Toni Wolff postulated a quaternary scheme embracing these types and two others, the Amazon and the medial woman: "Structural Forms of the Feminine Psyche," tr. Paul Watzlawik (Students Association, C. G. Jung Institute, Zurich, 1956). Cf. Wolff, *Studien zu C. G. Jungs Psychologie* (Zurich, 1959), pp. 269–83.

[13] Cf. Daudet's *L'Hérédo: Essai sur le drame intérieur* (1916), cited in "The Relations between the Ego and the Unconscious" (1928), CW 7, pars. 233, 270.

at night because one is then passive. However, with a dementia prae-cox patient it can be observed how the dreams come to the surface even in the daytime, because these people are passive all the time, so to speak, and simply turn themselves over to the dream life. A think-ing man's mind is active during the day (and remember I am speak-ing now exclusively of men; the process is different in women), but no dreams can be caught in this state. By assuming a passive attitude at night, while at the same time pouring the same stream of libido into the unconscious that one has put into work in the day, the dreams can be caught and the performances of the unconscious ob-served. But it cannot be done by just lying down on a couch and re-laxing, it has to be done by a definite giving over of the libido in full sum to the unconscious. I trained myself to do this; I gave all my libido to the unconscious in order to make it work, and in this way I gave the unconscious a chance, the material came to light and I was able to catch it *in flagrante*.

I found that the unconscious is working out enormous collective fantasies. Just as, before, I was passionately interested in working out myths, now I became just as much interested in the material of the unconscious. This in fact is the only way of getting at myth formation. And so the first chapter of the *Psychology of the Unconscious* became most correctly true. I watched the creation of myths going on, and got an insight into the structure of the unconscious, forming thus the concept that plays such a role in the *Types*. I drew all my empirical material from my patients, but the solution of the problem I drew from the inside, from my observations of the unconscious processes. I have tried to fuse these two currents of outer and inner experience in the book of the *Types*, and have termed the process of the fusion of the two currents the transcendent function.[14] I found that the con-scious current went one way and the unconscious another, and I could not see where they could become together. The individual tends toward an abysmal split, for the intellect can only dissect and discriminate, and the creative element lies out of reach of the intellect in the unconscious. The possibility of a mediation between the con-scious and the unconscious, which I have formulated in the transcen-dent function, came as a great light.

Now the time is up and I have told you a very great deal, but do not assume that I have told all!

[14] Cf. CW 6, pars. 184, 828.

LECTURE 5

20 April 1925

No written questions were handed in. The following verbal question was asked: "When you were in the process of investigating the unconscious, as you described it last time, did you have always the sense of being in control of your tools?"

Dr. Jung: It was as if my tools were activated by my libido. But there must be tools there to be activated, that is, animated images, images with libido in them; then the additional libido that one supplies brings them up to the surface. If I had not given this additional libido with which to bring them to the surface, the activity would have gone on just the same, but would have sucked my energy down into the unconscious. By putting libido into it, one can increase the speaking power of the unconscious.

Mr. Aldrich: Is that *tapas*?

Dr. Jung: Yes, that is the Indian term for that type of concentration. A further elaboration of the method might be put in this way: Suppose someone has a fantasy of a man and a woman moving about in a room. He gets just that far with it and no further; in other words, he drops that fantasy and proceeds to another—let us say he comes upon a deer in a wood, or sees birds fluttering about. But the technical rule with regard to fantasy is to stick to the picture that comes up until all its possibilities are exhausted. Thus if I conjured up that man and woman, I would not let them go till I had found out what they were going to do in that room. Thus one makes the fantasy move on. Usually, however, one has a resistance to doing this, that is, to following the fantasy. Something is sure to whisper in one's ear that it is all nonsense; in fact, the conscious is forced to take a highly depreciatory attitude toward the unconscious material in order to become conscious at all. Thus, for example, a person making the effort

35

to break away from an outgrown faith can usually be found ridiculing it; he throws out cogs to keep from slipping back into his unconscious acceptance. This is the reason it is so difficult to get at the unconscious material. The conscious is forever saying, "Keep away from all that," and it is always tending to increase rather than reduce the resistance to the unconscious. Similarly, the unconscious pits itself against the conscious, and it is the special tragedy of man that in order to win consciousness he is forced into dissociation with nature. He is either under the complete sway of the enantiodromia, or play of nature's forces, or he is too far away from nature.

Going back to the question of fantasizing, if once the resistance to free contact with the unconscious can be overcome, and one can develop the power of sticking to the fantasy, then the play of the images can be watched. Any artist is doing that quite naturally, but he is getting only the esthetic values out of it while the analyst tries to get at all the values, ideational, esthetic, feeling, and intuitional.

When one watches such a scene one tries to figure out its special meaning for oneself. When the figures animated are very far away from the conscious trend, then it may happen that they break forth arbitrarily as in cases of dementia praecox. The eruption then splits the conscious and tears it to bits, leaving each content with an independent ego, hence the absolutely inadequate emotional reaction of these cases. If there is a certain amount of ego left there may be some reaction—thus a voice in the unconscious may denounce one as crazy, but another may arise to counter it.

But, aside from dementia praecox cases, so-called normal people are very fragmentary—that is, they produce no full reactions in most cases. That is to say, they are not complete egos. There is one ego in the conscious and another made up of unconscious ancestral elements, by the force of which a man who has been fairly himself over a period of years suddenly falls under the sway of an ancestor. I think the fragmentary reactions and inadequate emotions people so often display are best explained along these lines. Thus you may have a person who sees always and only the dark side of life; he perhaps is forced into this one-sidedness through ancestor possession, and quite suddenly another portion of the unconscious may get on top and change him into an equally one-sided optimist. Many cases are described in the literature which show these sudden character changes, but of course they are not explained as ancestor possession, since this latter idea remains as a hypothesis for which there is no scientific proof as yet.

36

Following these ideas a little further, it is an interesting fact that there is no disease among primitives which cannot be caused by ghosts, which of course are ancestral figures.

There is a physiological analogy for this theory of ancestor possession which may make the idea a little clearer. It is thought that cancer may be due to the later and anarchical development of embryonic cells folded away in the mature and differentiated tissues. Strong evidence for this lies in the finding, for example, of a partially developed fetus in the thigh of an adult man, say, in those tumors known as teratomata. Perhaps a similar thing goes on in the mind, whose psychological makeup may be said to be a conglomerate. Perhaps certain traits belonging to the ancestors get buried away in the mind as complexes with a life of their own which has never been assimilated into the life of the individual, and then, for some unknown reason, these complexes become activated, step out of their obscurity in the folds of the unconscious, and begin to dominate the whole mind.

I am inclined to describe the historical character of the images from the unconscious in this way. Often there occur details in these images that cannot by any stretch of the imagination be explained in terms of the personal experience of the individual. It is possible that a certain historical atmosphere is born with us by means of which we can repeat strange details almost as if they were historical facts. Daudet has developed a similar idea (*L'Hérédo* and *Le Monde des images*), which he calls "auto-fécondation."[1] Whatever the truth of these speculations, they certainly fall within the frame of the notion of the collective unconscious.

Another way of putting these ideas of ancestor possession would be that these autonomous complexes exist in the mind as Mendelian units, which are passed on from generation to generation intact, and are unaffected by the life of the individual. The problem then becomes this: Can these psychological Mendelian units be broken up and assimilated in a way to protect the individual from being victimized by them? Analysis certainly makes a fair attempt to do this. It may not achieve the complete assimilation of the complex, or unit, into the rest of the mind, but at least it points out a way of dealing with it. In this way analysis becomes an orthopedic method analogous to that used in a disease like tabes, for example. The disease remains the same, but certain adjustments can be developed to compensate for the kinesthetic disturbance—the tabetic can learn to control his

[1] Cf. above, Lecture 4, n. 13.

body movements in walking, through his eye movements, and thus achieve a substitute for his lost tactile sense.

LECTURE

Í would like today to speak further about the background for the book on the types.

As soon as one begins to watch one's mind, one begins to observe the autonomous phenomena in which one exists as a spectator, or even as a victim. It is very much as if one stepped out of the protection of his house into an antediluvian forest and was confronted by all the monsters that inhabit the latter. One is naturally a little reluctant to reverse the machinery and get into this situation. It is as though one gave up one's freedom of will and offered oneself up as a victim, for with this reversal of the machinery, an entirely different attitude from that of directed thinking grows up. One is swept into the unknown of this world, not just into a psychological function. In a way the collective unconscious is merely a mirage because unconscious, but it can be also just as real as the tangible world. I can say this is so, this thing I am experiencing, but it does no good. One must be willing to accept the reality for the time being, to risk going a long way with the unconscious in other words. I once read some stories by the German author Hoffmann,[2] who wrote at the beginning of the nineteenth century. He wrote in the vein of Poe, and in the midst of writing these stories he would become so gripped by the reality of the fantasies that he would shout for help and have people running to his rescue. In fairly normal cases there is no danger, but it cannot be denied that the unconscious is overwhelmingly impressive.

The first observation I made began before I really had begun any systematic attempt to examine my unconscious—before I was fully aware of the full significance of the problem.

You remember what I told you of my relation to Freud. When I was still writing the *Psychology of the Unconscious*, I had a dream which I did not understand—perhaps I only fully understood it last year, if then. This was the dream: I was walking on a road in the country and came to a crossing. I was walking with someone, but did not know who it was—today I would say it was my shadow. Suddenly I came upon a man, an old one, in the uniform of an Austrian customs offi-

---

[2] E.T.A. Hoffmann, *The Devil's Elixir* (1813) and *The Golden Pot* (1813).

cial. It was Freud. In the dream the idea of the censorship came to my mind. Freud didn't see me but walked away silently. My shadow said to me, "Did you notice him? He has been dead for thirty years, but he can't die properly." I had a very peculiar feeling with this. Then the scene changed and I was in a southern town on the slopes of mountains. The streets consisted of steps going up and down the steep slopes. It was a medieval town and the sun was blazing in full noon, which as you know is the hour when spirits are abroad in southern countries. I came walking through the streets with my man, and many people passed us to and fro. All at once I saw among them a very tall man, a Crusader dressed in a coat of mail with the Maltese cross in red on the breast and on the back. He looked quite detached and aloof, not in any way concerned with the people about him, nor did they pay any attention to him. I looked at him in astonishment and could not understand what he was doing walking about there. "Did you notice him?" my shadow asked me. "He has been dead since the twelfth century, but he is not yet properly dead. He always walks here among the people, but they don't see him." I was quite bewildered that the people paid no attention, and then I awoke.[3]

This dream bothered me a long time. I was shocked at the first part because I did not then anticipate the trouble with Freud. "What does it mean that he is dead and so depreciated?" is the question I asked myself, and why did I think of the principle of the censor in these terms when, as a matter of fact, it seemed to me then the best theory available? I realized the antagonism between the figure of the Crusader and that of Freud, and yet I realized that there was also a strong parallelism. They were different, and yet both were dead and could not die properly.

The meaning of the dream lies in the principle of the ancestral figure; not the Austrian officer—obviously he stood for the Freudian theory—but the other, the Crusader, is an archetypal figure, a Christian symbol living from the twelfth century, a symbol that does not really live today, but on the other hand is not wholly dead either. It comes out of the times of Meister Eckhart,[4] the time of the culture of the Knights, when many ideas blossomed, only to be killed then, but they are coming again to life now. However, when I had this dream, I did not know this interpretation. I was oppressed and bewildered.

[3] Cf. *MDR*, pp. 163–65/158–60.

[4] German mystic and theologian, 13–14th cent., whom Jung read in his youth; cf. *MDR*, p. 68/76: "Only in Meister Eckhart did I feel the breath of life." Discussed extensively in *Types* (CW 6), pars. 410–33.

Freud was bewildered too, and could find no satisfactory meaning for
it.

That was in 1912. Then I had another dream that showed me
again very clearly the limitations of the conceptions about dreams
which Freud held to be final. I had been looking on the unconscious
as nothing but the receptacle of dead material, but slowly the idea of
the archetypes began to formulate itself in my mind, and at the end
of 1912 came this dream, which was the beginning of a conviction
that the unconscious did not consist of inert material only, but that
there was something living down there. I was greatly excited at the
idea of there being something living in me that I did not know anything about.

I dreamed that I was sitting in a very beautiful Italian loggia, something like the Palazzo Vecchio in Florence.[5] It was most luxurious,
with columns, floor, and balustrade of marble. I was sitting in a
golden chair, a Renaissance chair, in front of a table of green stone
like emerald. It was of an extraordinary beauty. I was sitting looking
out into space, for the loggia was on top of a tower belonging to a
castle. I knew that my children were there too. Suddenly a white bird
came flying down and gracefully alighted on the table. It was like a
small gull, or a dove. I made a sign to the children to keep quiet, and
the dove suddenly became a little girl with golden hair, and ran away
with the children. As I sat pondering over this, the little girl came
back and put her arm around my neck very tenderly. Then all at once
she was gone, and the dove was there and spoke slowly with a human
voice. It said, "I am allowed to transform into a human form only in
the first hours of the night, while the male dove is busy with the
twelve dead." Then it flew away into the blue sky and I awoke.

The dove had used a peculiar word when speaking of the male
dove. It is *Tauber* in German, and not often used, but I remembered
hearing an uncle of mine use it. But what should a male pigeon be
doing with twelve dead? I felt alarmed. Then there flashed across my
mind the story of the *Tabula smaragdina*, or emerald table, which is
part of the legend of the Thrice Great Hermes. He is supposed to
have left a table on which was engraved all the wisdom of the ages,
formulated in the Greek words: "Ether above, Ether below, Heaven
above, Heaven below, all this above, all this below, take it and be

---

[5] Cf. *MDR*, pp. 171f./166f. Chapter VI draws upon this lecture and the next one,
though the material there is more fully developed. / The comparison with the Palazzo
Vecchio is omitted in *MDR*. An adjacent building, the Loggia dei Lanzi, would better
serve the comparison.

happy."[6] All this, as I say, was very alarming to me. I began to think of the twelve Apostles, the twelve months of the year, the signs of the Zodiac, etc. I had just written about the twelve signs of the Zodiac in the *Psychology of the Unconscious*. Finally, I had to give it up, I could make nothing out of the dream except that there was a tremendous animation of the unconscious. I knew no technique of getting at the bottom of this activity; all I could do was just wait, keep on living, and watch the fantasies.

This was at Christmastime in 1912. In 1913 I felt the activity of the unconscious most disagreeably. I was disturbed, but knew nothing better to do than to try to analyze my infantile memories. So I began to analyze these most conscientiously, but found nothing. I thought, "Well then, I must try to live through these experiences again," so I made then the effort to recover the emotional tone of childhood. I said to myself that if I should play like a child I could recover this. I remembered that when I was a boy I used to delight in building houses of stone, all sorts of fantastic castles, churches, and towns.[7] "For Heaven's sake," I said to myself, "is it possible that I have to get into this nonsense for the sake of animating the unconscious?" That year I did all sorts of idiotic things like this, and enjoyed them like a fool. It raised a lot of inferior feelings in me, but I knew of no better way. Towards autumn I felt that the pressure that had seemed to be within me was not there anymore but in the air. The air actually seemed darker than before. It was just as if it were no longer a psychological situation in which I was involved, but a real one, and that sense became more and more weighty.

In October 1913 I was travelling in a train and had a book in my hand that I was reading. I began to fantasize, and before I knew it, I was in the town to which I was going. This was the fantasy: I was looking down on the map of Europe in relief. I saw all the northern part, and England sinking down so that the sea came in upon it. It came up to Switzerland, and then I saw that the mountains grew higher and higher to protect Switzerland. I realized that a frightful catastrophe was in progress, towns and people were destroyed, and the wrecks and dead bodies were tossing about on the water. Then the whole sea turned to blood. At first I was only looking on dispassionately, and then the sense of the catastrophe gripped me with tremendous power. I tried to repress the fantasy, but it came again and

---

[6] Jung quotes this saying in *Wandlungen und Symbole* (cf. *Psychology of the Unconscious*, 1916 ed., p. 63), attributing it only to "the old mystic." Repeating it in CW 5, par. 77, he fully cites the *Tabula* and Hermes.

[7] Cf. *MDR*, pp. 173f./168f.

held me bound for two hours. Three or four weeks later it came again, when I was again in a train. It was the same picture repeated, only the blood was more emphasized.[8]

Of course I asked myself if I was so unfortunate as to be spreading my personal complexes all over Europe. I thought a great deal about the chances of a great social revolution, but curiously enough never of a war. It seemed to me all these things were becoming frightfully uncanny, then it occurred to me, there was something I could do, I could write down all of it in sequence. While I was writing once I said to myself, "What is this I am doing, it certainly is not science, what is it?" Then a voice said to me, "That is art." This made the strangest sort of an impression upon me, because it was not in any sense my conviction that what I was writing was art. Then I came to this, "Perhaps my unconscious is forming a personality that is not me, but which is insisting on coming through to expression." I don't know why exactly, but I knew to a certainty that the voice that had said my writing was art had come from a woman.[9] A living woman could very well have come into the room and said that very thing to me, because she would not have cared anything about the discriminations she was trampling underfoot. Obviously it wasn't science; what then could it be but art, as though those were the only two alternatives in the world. That is the way a woman's mind works.

Well, I said very emphatically to this voice that what I was doing was not art, and I felt a great resistance grow up within me. No voice came through, however, and I kept on writing. Then I got another shot like the first: "That is art." This time I caught her and said, "No it is not," and I felt as though an argument would ensue. I thought, well, she has not the speech centers I have, so I told her to use mine, and she did, and came through with a long statement.

This is the origin of the technique I developed for dealing directly with the unconscious contents.

[8] Ibid., pp. 175f./169f. Cf. Jung's painting (later) in *Jung: Word and Image*, p. 57.

[9] *MDR*, pp. 185ff./178ff., following several pages in which Jung describes other dreams and visions. At this point he wrote, "I knew for a certainty that the voice had come from a woman. I recognized it as the voice of a patient, a talented psychopath who had a strong transference to me." It has been speculated that this was Sabina Spielrein. Cf. Aldo Carotenuto, *A Secret Symmetry: Sabina Spielrein between Jung and Freud*, tr. John Shepley, Krishna Winston, et al. (New York, 2nd ed., 1984), p. 211; and *Freud/Jung*, index, s.v. "Spielrein." Also cf. *MDR*, p. 195/186: "toward the end of the First World War . . . I broke with the woman who was determined to convince me that my fantasies had artistic value." Carotenuto, p. 190, cites one of Jung's last letters to Spielrein, dated 1 Sept. 1919.

LECTURE 6

27 April 1925

Dr. Harding asked for more discussion of the personal aspects of the fantasy given by Dr. Jung in the last lecture.

Dr. Jung: I could be taken as Switzerland fenced in by mountains, and the submergence of the world could be the debris of my former relationships. You remember that when I tried to describe the condition surrounding the fantasy I spoke of the peculiar feeling I had had of the thing being atmospheric. But here one proceeds with the utmost caution. If I were a case of dementia praecox I would easily spread my dreams over the whole world and take it that the destruction of the world was indicated, whereas in reality all that might be indicated would be the destruction of my relation to the world. A person with dementia praecox wakes up one day to find that the world is dead and the doctor nothing but a ghost—he alone is alive and right. But in such cases there are always plenty of other symptoms present to prove the essential abnormality of the person. The more normal the individual, the more it can be assumed from such fantasies that some profound social disturbance actually is in progress, and at such times there are always many more than one person whose unconsciouses register the upset conditions.

When the unconscious produces such a fantasy the personal contents are given an impersonal aspect, there being in the unconscious a tendency to produce collective pictures that make the connection with mankind in general. One sees this process going on in dementia praecox and paranoia perfectly clearly. It is precisely because these people often have fantasies and dreams that are collectively valid that they get followers. First they make a break with the world through their morbidity, then comes the revelation of a special mission, and then they begin to preach. People think them thrilling personalities,

43

and women feel it a tremendous honor to have children by them. By primitives they are imagined to be full of gods and ghosts.

So if I had been crazy, I could have preached the coming disaster like the man on the walls of Jerusalem.

Mrs. Zinno: Were these fantasies full of affect?

Dr. Jung: Yes, there was a great deal of affect with them. As I could see no possible application to be made of them, I thought to myself, "If this means anything, it means that I am hopelessly off." I had the feeling that I was an over-compensated psychosis, and from this feeling I was not released till August 1st, 1914.

LECTURE[1]

I told you last time how I began to train myself in making communications with split-off portions of the unconscious. As I said, I was sure this voice that gave me the absurd dictum about my writing being art was undoubtedly a woman, though I could not know why. I was much interested in the fact that a woman should interfere with me from within. My conclusion was that it must be the soul in the primitive sense, and I began to speculate on the reasons that the name "anima" was given to the soul. Why was it thought of as feminine? What she said to me I found to be full of a deep cunning. There I was, writing autobiographical material, but not as an autobiography—there was no style in it, I simply wanted to have it down in writing. Then came this remark as though I were writing a novel. I thought this so wrong that I got angry with her. Inasmuch as it manifestly was not scientific, I might have taken it for art, but I knew perfectly well that this was a wrong attitude. With a secret conviction that it was art, I could easily have watched the course of the unconscious as I would watch a cinema. If I read a certain book I may become deeply moved by it, but after all, it is all outside myself; and in the same way if I had taken these dreams and fantasies from the unconscious as art, I would have had from them only a perceptional conviction, and would have felt no moral obligation toward them. Take, for example, this way I found of getting to know the anima; I could have looked down upon this phenomenon as from a pedestal, and in that way I would have become identified with the unconscious, and would have become its plaything. From the trouble it took me to

[1] Cf. *MDR*, chapter VI, "Confrontation with the Unconscious."

put up with the interference I had from this anima figure, I could measure the power of the unconscious, and it was great indeed.

In the same way that the anima played this trick of cunning insinuation upon me, giving a false slant to the situation and tempting me away from a reality grasp of it, so the animus can work in the mind of a woman. He comes as a conviction before there is any justification in having a conviction, and throws things out of plumb, though often in such a delicate way that it takes the utmost subtlety to run him down to his lair. My anima could easily have worked me up to the state of believing that I was a misunderstood artist, privileged to cast aside reality for the sake of pursuing these alleged artistic gifts. If I had followed my unconscious along these lines, one fine day my anima would have come and said to me, "Do you imagine this nonsense you are doing is art? It is nothing of the sort." Thus one can be ground to pieces in an enantiodromia phenomenon. Following uncritically the unconscious turns one, as I have said, into the plaything of the unconscious opposites. These unconscious pulls contain an extraordinary intensity. There is energy and a certain amount of adaptation to the actual facts in them, but when examined critically, they can always be found to be beside the mark.

The experience I described is not the only one of its kind that I had. Often [when] writing I would have peculiar reactions that threw me off. Slowly I learned to distinguish between myself and the interruption. When something vulgar or banal comes in, I must say to myself, it is perfectly true that I have thought in this stupid way at some time or other, but I don't have to think that way now; I must not accept this stupidity as mine in perpetuity—for that is an unnecessary humiliation. If I just tell the anima that she is working off some collective notion on me which I have no idea of accepting as part of my individuality, that does no good at all—when I am in the grip of an emotion it is no support to me to say it is a collective reaction. But if you can isolate these unconscious phenomena by personifying them, that is a technique that works for stripping them of power. It is not too much of a stretch of the imagination to personify them, for they have always a certain degree of separateness. This separateness is a most uncomfortable thing to reconcile oneself to, and yet the very fact of the unconscious presenting itself that way gives us the means of handling it. It took me a long time to adapt to something in myself that was not myself—that is, to the fact that there were in my individual mind parts that did not pertain to me.

After this I began to work on the problem already ancient in the world, "Has woman a soul?" I decided she could not possibly have an anima, because then there would be no check on the woman from within. Then I came to the idea that woman must have an animus, but it was not till much later that I was able to develop this further because the animus is much harder to catch at work.

These ideas about the animus and the anima led me ever further afield into metaphysical problems, and more things crept up for reexamination. At that time I was on the Kantian basis that there were things that could never be solved and that therefore should not be speculated about, but it seemed to me if I could find such definite ideas about the anima, it was quite worthwhile to try to formulate a conception of God. But I could arrive at nothing satisfactory and thought for a time that perhaps the anima figure was the deity. I said to myself that perhaps men had had a female God originally, but, growing tired of being governed by women, they had then overthrown this God. I practically threw the whole metaphysical problem into the anima and conceived of it as the dominating spirit of the psyche. In this way I got into a psychological argument with myself about the problem of God.

At first it was the negative aspect of the anima that most impressed me. I felt a little awed by her. It was like the feeling of an invisible presence in the room one enters. Then a new idea came to me: In putting down all this material for analysis, I was in effect writing letters to my anima, that is to a part of myself with a different viewpoint from my own. I got remarks of a new character—I was in analysis with a ghost and a woman. Every evening I wrote very conscientiously for I thought if I did not write it, there would be no way for the anima to get at it. There is a tremendous difference in the assumption of telling something and the actual telling of it, a fact which I was once able to test out experimentally. I told a man whom I was testing to think of something disagreeable, but to let it be something I did not know about. I took his electric resistance in the so-called psycho-galvanic experiment,[2] and there was very little change. In some way I knew that he was thinking about something very disagreeable that had happened that morning, but something which I had found out only by accident, and of which he was confident I knew nothing. I said to him, "Now I will tell you what that disagreeable thing was," and as soon as I told him I got a tremendous reaction in the current.

[2] Cf. the psychophysical researches (1907–1908) in CW 2.

For the sake then of trying to achieve the maximum of honesty with myself, I wrote everything down very carefully,[3] following the old Greek mandate: "Give away all thou possessest, then thou shalt receive." The writing of this material took me into November 1913, and then I came to an end of it. Not knowing what would come next, I thought perhaps more introspection was needed. When we introspect we look within and see if there is anything to be observed, and if there is nothing we may either give up the introspective process or find a way of "boring through" to the material that escapes the first survey. I devised such a boring method by fantasizing that I was digging a hole, and by accepting this fantasy as perfectly real.[4] This is naturally somewhat difficult to do—to believe so thoroughly in a fantasy that it leads you into further fantasy, just as if you were digging a real hole and passing from one discovery to another. But when I began on that hole I worked and worked so hard that I knew something had to come of it—that fantasy had to produce, and lure out, other fantasies.

Of course, in using a hole I was using an archetype of considerable power in stimulating the unconscious, for the mystery attaching to caves comes down from immemorial times; one thinks at once of the Mithraic cult, of the catacombs, etc. Why do we have a peculiar feeling on entering a cathedral? Just because it is an archetypal situation that has always aroused the unconscious of man. I had just such a feeling of awe when I saw the Grand Canyon of the Colorado;[5] it had to be like that, and my unconscious was touched in a peculiar way. So the more I worked on this fantasy hole, the more I seemed to descend. Finally I felt I had to come to a place where I could go no further down. I said to myself that, that being the case, I would then go horizontally, and then it seemed as if I were in a corridor, and as though I were wading in black slime. I went in, thinking to myself that this was the remnant of an old mine.

Far ahead, I could see a dim red light, and following this I came to a cave full of insects, bat-like in form, and making a strange noise. I saw in one end of the cave a rock, and on the rock was a light, a

---

[3] Cf. *MDR*, p. 188/180: "I wrote these fantasies down first in the Black Book; later, I transferred them to the Red Book, which I also embellished with drawings." Some of the drawings (rather, paintings) are reproduced in *Jung: Word and Image*, pp. 67–75.

[4] Cf. *MDR*, pp. 179f./172f., where the fantasy is described in detail.

[5] Jung had visited the Grand Canyon on New Year's Day, 1925, with a party of friends. Cf. McGuire, "Jung in America," pp. 39ff., and Barbara Hannah, *Jung, His Life and Work: A Biographical Memoir* (New York, 1976), pp. 158ff.

luminous crystal. "Ah," I said, "that's it." I took it up in my hand and found it was like a ruby. Where it had been there was a hole which it had covered. Forgetting now entirely that I was making a fantasy, I said to myself, "How curious to put a crystal over a hole." I looked into the hole, and then I could hear the noise of rushing water. I was shocked, and as I peered further down, in the dim light I could see something floating, the body of a fair-haired man. I thought at once, "That is the hero!" Then there came floating past a big black something nearly as big as the body of the man and coming after him with moving legs. This was a scarab, and after it came a ball that was like a luminous sun, glowing dark red in the waters like a sunrise before a storm. When it was in the middle of the field of vision, hundreds of thousands of snakes threw themselves on the sun and obscured it.

I withdrew from the hole, and then blood came gushing from it as from a severed artery. I had a most disagreeable feeling. The blood kept gushing up and would not stop. I had the feeling of being absolutely powerless, and I was utterly exhausted.

When I came out of the fantasy, I realized that my mechanism had worked wonderfully well, but I was in great confusion as to the meaning of all those things I had seen. The light in the cave from the crystal was, I thought, like the stone of wisdom. The secret murder of the hero I could not understand at all. The beetle of course I knew to be an ancient sun symbol, and the setting sun, the luminous red disk, was archetypal. The serpents I thought might have been connected with Egyptian material. I could not then realize that it was all so archetypal, I need not seek connections. I was able to link the picture up with the sea of blood I had previously fantasized about.

Though I could not then grasp the significance of the hero killed, soon after I had a dream in which Siegfried was killed by myself.[6] It was a case of destroying the hero ideal of my efficiency. This has to be sacrificed in order that a new adaptation can be made; in short, it is connected with the sacrifice of the superior function in order to get at the libido necessary to activate the inferior functions. If a man has a good brain, thinking becomes his hero and, instead of Christ, Kant, or Bergson, becomes his ideal. If you give up this thinking, this hero ideal, you commit a secret murder—that is, you give up your superior function.

With all of this I give you the impure thoughts that lay back of the *Types*, where I have carried over into abstract terms the contest be-

[6] Cf. *MDR*, p. 180/173.

tween the superior and inferior functions, first seen by me in the symbolic form of the slaying of the hero. Such things as I have described in these fantasies speak in symbolic form of things later to become conscious and to take form as abstract thoughts, when they will look altogether different from their plastic origins. A similar case to mine is that of the famous chemist who discovered the so-called benzol "ring." He first visualized his theory of a ring as couples dancing in a peculiar way.[7]

[7] The German chemist F. A. Kekulé von Stradonitz proposed (1865) the ring structure of the benzene or benzol molecule supposedly after seeing such a form in a dream or vision. Jung's first published reference is in "The Visions of Zosimos" (1937; CW 13), par. 143. Cf. also "The Psychology of the Transference" (1946; CW 16), par. 353.

LECTURE 7

4 May 1925

Mrs. Zinno's question: "If the technique of introversion which you described be used before the pairs of opposites have been stretched to the uttermost in conflict, will the collective unconscious be constellated instead of the releasing symbol?"

Dr. Jung: It must not by any means be supposed that the technique described is suitable for general use or imitation. That would indeed be disastrous. It is something applicable to a particular case under particular circumstances, and is only applicable when the unconscious is animated, and when the unconscious content is necessary for further progress. There are very many cases in which the conscious material is in need of being digested, and in those cases it would be quite futile to call up the unconscious content. I can call to mind now a case where the analyst released the unconscious under wrong conditions, and with the most unfortunate results. In my own case the release of the unconscious was demanded. The conscious had become practically a *tabula rasa*, and the contents underneath had to be freed.

Dr. Mann: In speaking of the animus, one always does so in a derogatory way. I should like to hear a discussion of its positive value, but no doubt you will speak further about the animus later on.

Dr. Jung: Yes, on the whole I would rather defer this, but as a partial answer here I can say that the animus, being discovered as he usually is under the most unpleasant circumstances, suffers from the fact. Most psychological things are discovered that way because as long as things are running smoothly, no one thinks of trying to understand them. It is only when problems arise that we are forced into a conscious attitude toward our psychical processes. By being discovered chiefly under disagreeable circumstances, the animus comes into

50

ill repute, though of course it has a tremendously important positive function as presenting the relationship to the unconscious.

Similarly, "persona" has come into a bad name. No one can imagine getting along without a persona—that is, a relationship to the outside world—but when one identifies with the persona, its valuable side disappears in its abuse. So when one is all animus, one loses sight of the service the animus performs when it is held within its proper functioning limits.

Mrs. Zinno: In my question I had especially in mind the phenomenon one can see going on today in modern art—that is, the artist pumps his unconscious for the sake of the images he can find there and not for a psychological need, and so he brings out a lot of embryonic stuff instead of the releasing symbol.

Dr. Jung: This brings us into the problem of the significance of modern art. I'm not at all sure that all those present would agree modern art brought out embryonic material from the unconscious. What would you say to that, Mr. Aldrich?

Mr. Aldrich: I think modern art is too big a term for satisfactory discussion.

Dr. Jung: Limit it then to painting.

Mr. Aldrich: Some modern art has for me a really magic spell. For example, not long ago I saw in Lugano[1] a painting of a bull and a man struggling with it. The background was flat blue, with six points of light set in it—six stars or planets, so that the man and the bull seemed to suggest that they were the seventh. The bull was not like any bull that exists on the earth today; he was antique; he was not just a bull, he was The Bull. So too with the human figure: there was no effort at portraiture or photographic rendering of a man—he was more than any one man, he was Man. There was a sense of tremendous power and space. The Bull swept past the stars dragging with him Man who strove to dominate him. The artist—I questioned him—had never even heard of Mithras and the bull: the picture was pure fantasy that had come up from the unconscious. Another example is a painting that was in the Kunsthaus here,[2] a great black horse rearing up, wild with demoniac energy. On his back sat a heroic figure of a man armed with a spear, nude except for a helmet, who

---

[1] Unidentified. The famous Thyssen-Bornemisza collection was installed at the Villa Favorita, in Lugano, only in 1932.

[2] Presumably J. H. Füssli (Henry Fuseli), *Huon's Encounter with Sherasmin in the Cave of Lebanon* (1804–1805), private collection, Winterthur (Switzerland); sometimes exhibited at the Kunsthaus, Zurich.

seemed to look intently ahead into the far distance. He was undisturbed by the ferocity of his horse. This horse, like The Bull, was no particular animal—rather, he was The Horse. Both these pictures stirred me greatly.

Dr. Jung: Why did they stir you? If you could answer that it would explain the appeal of modern art.

Mr. Aldrich: I think they were libido symbols, and that the struggle with the bull, for instance, pictured the conflict in man's soul.

Dr. Jung: Was there any difference between those pictures and one painted 150 or 200 years ago?

Mr. Aldrich: Yes, a very great difference. I could see a picture of a peasant's horse painted in the old way, and while I would know it to be an excellent painting, it would not stir me.

Dr. Jung: That is just it. The criterion of art is that it grips you. Constable no longer does this to us, but undoubtedly he did stir the people of his time. Most probably the art produced now would be anathema to our ancestors. It would have no value for them. One has to assume, I think, that the artist adapts to the change of attitude.

Now I should be most interested to hear the views of the class on this theme of art.

One can take art as a form of dream. Just as the dream seeks to maintain a psychological balance by filling out the daytime conscious attitude by the unconscious elements, so art balances the general public tendency of a given time. What do you think about art from that viewpoint?

Mrs. Zinno: Is not the characteristic thing of modern art that it is subjective?

Dr. Jung: But if you say that, you must be very careful to define what you mean by subjective. Very often it is assumed that an experience is subjective because it takes place within the mind of a subject, but it is not then necessarily in opposition to objective, because the images of the collective unconscious, from their collective character, are just as truly objects as things outside the psyche. Now, I think modern art tends to be subjective in the sense that the artist is concerned with his individual connection with the object, rather than with the object *per se*.

It is perfectly true that modern art also tends toward an increased interest in the inner object, but that does not in itself, as I have just said, constitute subjectivity. In modern art one feels decidedly the predomination of the internal processes. To take the examples Mr. Aldrich gave, we could say that these artists were more interested in the image of the horse or bull than in any actual animals, and still more interested in their relation to those images. But what then is the aim of art? An artist would instantly resent that question and would say that art is just art when it has no aim.

Miss Baynes: Is it not the aim of art to counteract the effects of machinery on modern life?

Mr. Bacon: Does it not do something for the artist?

Dr. Jung: Undoubtedly both of these points of view are true, but then there must be something over and above that.

Dr. de Angulo: I think modern art is a misplaced effort to balance the extreme to which scientific thought has forced modern man. I say misplaced because the artist is almost driven into a morbid extreme, and "puts it up" to his public to make the connection between his product and the conscious viewpoint.

Dr. Jung: Many would certainly contest the point that modern art is morbid.

Mr. Aldrich: It seems to me that a characteristic thing of modern art is that it no longer concerns itself with being merely beautiful. It has passed through and beyond mere conventional beauty, and in this it reflects our changed views of life. Before the war we lived in a beautiful world—or perhaps I would better say in a world that was merely sweet and pretty, a world of sticky sentimentality in which nothing brutal nor ugly was given place. Modern art certainly cares nothing for prettiness; in fact, it would rather have the ugly than the pretty; and sometimes, I think, it seeks a new realization of beauty beyond the pale of what was formerly considered possible—in ugliness itself, even.

(There followed here some discussion in the class as to whether modern art had really freed us from sentimentalism, or merely shifted the kind of sentimentalism a little.)

Dr. Jung: There is no doubt that sentimentalism catches the public and blinds it to its own sensuality and brutality. Thus in the time of Louis XVI, one had all those beautiful shepherdesses and idylls of one sort or another in France, and then followed the Revolution. Or again, we can see the raw hell of war coming after the purity and exaggerated delicacy of feeling of the Victorian age, when a lady and a gentleman neither spoke nor thought anything evil. All through history one can see periods of pronounced brutality directly predicted by the sentimentality of the art preceding them. And the same thing, of course, goes on in the case of the individual artist—that is, he uses sentimentality to cloak brutality. These two seem to be opposites between which an enantiodromia works.

Mrs. Zinno: Is not the best expression of modern art to be found in sculpture?

Dr. Jung: No, because sculpture demands form, and form [demands] an idea, while painting can dispense with form. The cubistic sculpture seems to say all of[3] nothing. But in painting one can find the thread of development. For example, I once followed very carefully the course of Picasso's painting.[4] All of a sudden he was struck by the triangular shadow thrown by the nose on the cheek. Later on the cheek itself became a four-sided shadow, and so it went. These triangles and squares became nuclei with independent values of their own, and the human figure gradually disappeared, or became dissolved in space.

There was once exhibited in New York a painting called the *Nude Descending the Stairs*.[5] This might be said to present a double dissolution of the object, that is in time and space, for not only have the figure and the stairs gone over into the triangles and squares, but the figure is up and down the stairs at the same time, and it is only by moving the picture that one can get the figure to come out as it would in an ordinary painting where the artist preserved the integrity of the figure in space and time. The essence of this process is the depreciation of the object. It is a somewhat similar performance such as that we go through when we cast aside the reality of a living man and reduce him to his infantile misdeeds. The artist takes the object away from our eyes, and substitutes a partial derivative. It is no longer a nose but its shadow we are shown. Or, to put it another way, he shifts the emphasis from the essential to the unessential. It is a little bit as though you explained a thing by a *bon mot*, a fugitive exhalation of the thing.

This process inevitably drives the interest away from the object to the subject, and instead of the real object, the internal object becomes the carrier of the values. It is Plato's conception of the eidolon coming again to the fore. Thus, when the artist paints such a bull as that described by Mr. Aldrich, it is *the* bull he has painted, it is yours or

---

3 *Sic.* Perhaps a transcribing slip for "or"?

4 Cf. the essay "Picasso" (1932; CW 15), pars. 204ff.

5 The French painter Marcel Duchamp's *Nude Descending a Staircase* created a furor when exhibited at the Armory Show in New York, 17 Feb.–15 Mar. 1913. Jung was in New York during mid-March; cf. *Freud/Jung*, 350 J, n. 1. Also at the Armory Show, he could have seen paintings by Picasso, presumably for the first time.

mine—God's bull, you might say. The Bull-Tamer is a collective idea of tremendous power gathered into an image. It speaks of discipline—only a man of heroic attributes overcomes the bull. So modern art leads us away from the too great scattering of the libido on the external object, back to the creative source within us, back to the inner values. In other words, it leads us by the same path analysis tries to lead us, only it is not a conscious leadership on the part of the artist.

We have analysis for exactly the purpose of getting us back to those inner values so little understood by the modern man. Analysis would have been unthinkable in the Middle Ages, because those men were freely expressing those values from which we have cut ourselves off today. Catholics today have no need of analysis because the unconscious in them is not constellated—it is kept perpetually drained through their ritual. The unconscious of a Catholic is empty.

I once made a collection of portraits carrying back through the Middle Ages, in order to trace the change in psychological attitude between the medieval man and ourselves. Down to the middle of the sixteenth century or thereabouts, these portraits are my relatives. I understand these men and women in the same sense that I understand my contemporaries. But in the middle of the sixteenth century a change begins and the Gothic man, the pre-Reformation man, comes on the scene, and he is a stranger to us. There is a very peculiar look about him, his eyes are stone-like and inexpressive; none of the vivacity to be seen in our eyes is in them. Sometimes one sees this face reproduced in modern times among peasants and people of the ignorant classes who have not awakened to modern life. Thus the cook of my mother-in-law has a perfect Gothic face, the arched eyebrows and pointed smile of the Madonna.

If you notice Luther's face you can find that he is not quite modern, but belonged to the time before the Reformation also. He has still in a way the Gothic look and the Gothic mouth.

There is combined in this smile the paranoid's idea of persecution, of martyrdom, and the sardonic smile of catatonia. It is also the smile of *Mona Lisa*. It is connected, too, with the antique smile as one sees it on the Aegina marbles,[6] those men who are enduring death with a smile. The Gothic smile is almost like the beginning of a kiss—full of tenderness, like a mother. Or it is the smile of a man who meets on

---

[6] The sculptures (5th cent. B.C.), in the Glyptothek, Munich, which depict scenes of the Trojan War.

the street the woman with whom he has a secret liaison. There is understanding in the smile—"We know," it seems to say.

I think these peculiarities of the Gothic attitude are to be explained by the fact that at one time there was one language, one belief, from north to south. The smile bespoke the complete conviction that excluded all doubt, therefore the kinship with the paranoid. All this disappeared with the advent of the modern viewpoint. The world broke into diversified faiths, and the inner unit and quietude gave place to the materialistic urge toward conquest of the outer world. Through science values became exteriorized.

Modern art, then, began first by depreciating these external values, by dissolving the object, and then sought the basic thing, the internal image back of the object—the eidolon. We can hardly predict today what the artist is going to bring forth, but always a great religion has gone hand in hand with a great art.

LECTURE

At the last lecture I told you of my descent into the cavern. After that came a dream in which I had to kill Siegfried. Siegfried was not an especially sympathetic figure to me, and I don't know why my unconscious got engrossed in him. Wagner's Siegfried, especially, is exaggeratedly extraverted and at times actually ridiculous. I never liked him. Nevertheless my dream showed him to be my hero. I could not understand the strong emotion I had with the dream. I can tell it here appropriately because it connects with the theme we have been discussing with respect to art, that is, with the change of values.

This was the dream:[7] I was in the Alps, not alone, but with another man, a curious shortish man with brown skin. Both of us carried rifles. It was just before dawn, when the stars were disappearing from the sky, and we were climbing up the mountain together. Suddenly I heard Siegfried's horn sound out from above, and I knew that it was he we were to shoot. The next minute he appeared high above us, lit up by a shaft of sunlight from the rising sun. He came plunging down the mountainside in a chariot made of bones. I thought to myself, "Only Siegfried could do that." Presently, around a bend in the trail, he came upon us, and we fired full into his breast. Then I was filled with horror and disgust at myself for the cowardice of what we

[7] Cf. *MDR*, pp. 179ff./173f.

had done. The little man with me went forward, and I knew he was going to drive the knife into Siegfried's heart, but that was just a little too much for me, and I turned and fled. I had the idea of getting away as fast as I could to a place where "they" could not find me. I had the choice of going down into the valley or further up the mountains by a faint trail. I chose the latter, and as I ran there broke upon me a perfect deluge of rain. Then I awoke with a sense of great relief.

The hero, as I told you, is the symbol of the greatest value recognized by us. Christ has been our hero when we accept the principles of his life as our own principles. Or Herakles or Mithras becomes my hero when I am determined to be as disciplined as they were. So it appeared as if Siegfried were my hero. I felt an enormous pity for him, as though I myself had been shot. I must then have had a hero I did not appreciate, and it was my ideal of force and efficiency I had killed. I had killed my intellect, helped on to the deed by a personification of the collective unconscious, the little brown man with me. In other words, I deposed my superior function.

The same thing is going on in art, that is, the killing of one function in order to release another.

The rain that fell is a symbol of the release of tension; that is, the forces of the unconscious are loosed. When this happens, the feeling of relief is engendered. The crime is expiated because, as soon as the main function is deposed, there is a chance for other sides of the personality to be born into life.

LECTURE 8

11 May 1925

Dr. Harding's question: "In your talk last time about art you used the term 'subjective.' There have been discussions between several of us in the group as to the significance of that term, and there seem to be as many views as there are disputants. In particular there seems to be a widespread idea that subjective is a term that can only be applied to the introvert, and on the other hand that an introvert cannot possess a concrete personality. Will you elucidate this for us?"

Dr. Jung: "Subjective" denotes in the first place just what you know it does, that is, the view of a given individual which is special to him and different from that of any other individual. In this sense it is often used as a criticism of an attitude, that is, as meaning that a person is not taking a given thing objectively, or "as it really is," as we say. But, of course, it need not be a reproach to say that an opinion is subjective. It might be that what is wanted is the particular individual's personal opinion.

Then the term "subjective" also means an argument coming from the subject, but nonetheless an object. In every person there are certain collective ideas—such, for example, as the Darwinian theory—which are quite objective. They in no sense belong to the subject simply because they are to be found in his mind. Again there are certain unconscious products which people like to think of as establishing forever the uniqueness of their individualities, but which in reality are shared by all and are, by reason of this collective quality, objects vis-à-vis the subject's mind.

It must of course be remembered that there is no objective statement that is not subjective to a certain extent. That is, it has undergone a certain degree of refraction by reason of its passage through the subject's mind. This was never so clear to me as when I was writing the *Types*. I found it well-nigh impossible to reduce the refraction

58

to the desired minimum. The minute a thing goes into language it is *ipso facto* conditioned in its objectivity. Take for example a German writing about feeling: It is a peculiarity of the German language that it does not distinguish between "sensation" and "feeling" [*Empfindung*] as do English and French. Therefore, a German writing about feeling is quite likely to say sensation instead of feeling and therefore to give his idea a slant absolutely peculiar to himself. But again, take the German word *Wirklichkeit*, "reality." The Latin word from which "reality" is derived is *res*, literally "thing." But the German translates "thing-reality" as *Dinglichkeit*, and *Wirklichkeit* means to him a special kind of reality, namely the reality of working, of validity in life. It would lead us into a terrible entanglement of subtleties if we traced out the further connotations included in these words, but you can see what a serious handicap language is when it comes to thoroughgoing objectivity. Thus the images in our mind tend to form prejudices, of a greater or less rigidity to be sure, but nevertheless prejudices from which we can never be wholly free. These preexisting mental images into contact with which the stream of our personal experience comes, I call the subjective factor. Our mental processes cannot escape the intermingling with these preexisting images, so it is easy to see why a new idea always has to fight for its life against these ancestral predispositions. You can tell a man a new idea and he says, "Yes, of course," and you are pleased with his understanding, but the chances are he has taken the idea and twisted every spark of life out of it in order to make it fit better the morgue of which his own mind consists; you finish by wishing you had never attempted to launch the idea.

The subjective factor, then, in this second sense, is held to be made up of objective material, namely ancestral views. The artist returns to these ancestral views. He leaves the outer object and returns to the object as seen by his mind rather than as seen by his senses. Does this answer your question, Dr. Harding?

Dr. Harding: Yes, but I would like it if you would make a closer connection between "subjective" and introversion and extraversion.

Dr. Jung: The extravert bases himself on the value of the outer object, the introvert on that of the inner object. The extravert is controlled by his relation to the thing without, the introvert by his relation to the thing within. Both of these attitudes grow out of attitudes to be found among primitive peoples, because to the primitive the inner and the outer tend to form one experience. The primitive is quite sure that he has both inner and outer value because it does not occur to him to distinguish between the two. The ancient gods were exteriorized emotions personified. It is only through consciousness that the discrimination between inner and outer experience is achieved, and only by consciousness that a man can know he is connected with the outer object to the neglect of the inner and vice versa.

The conscious extravert values his connection with the outer object and fears his own inner self. The introvert has no fear of himself, but great fear of the object, which he comes to endow with extraordinary terrors. You remember the story of Alcibiades and Socrates.[1] Alcibiades was due to make a public speech and came and told Socrates that he had failed to do it through fear of the audience. Socrates led him about Athens, and coming first to a blacksmith said, "Do you know this man?" "Yes." "Do you fear him?" "No." Then he took him to a shoemaker and asked the same questions, and again Alcibiades had no fear. "These," said Socrates, "are just the men before whom you were afraid to speak." But it is ordinarily that way for the introvert, the crowd heaping itself up into a monster before him. Sometimes he is able to compensate and to develop a very forceful manner in order to subdue the monster. The fear the introvert feels rests on the unconscious assumption that the object is too much animated, and this is a part of the ancient belief in magic.

The extravert, on the other hand, behaves as if the world were a lovely family. He does not project terrors into the object, but is quite at home with it. But to show you the way he feels about himself, I can tell you of a patient I had who was wearing himself out with extravagant extraversion. I told him he must take an hour apart each day when he would be quite by himself. He said it would be fine to have some music with his wife in the evening. "No," I said, "that is not it, you must be by yourself." "To read, you mean?" "No, to do nothing but think." "Not for anything in the world," he said. "That leads to straight-out melancholia."

Dr. de Angulo: If you were told that a person had an extraverted attitude toward the material of the collective unconscious, what would you take it to mean?

Dr. Jung: That is difficult to say. What do you think it means?

Dr. de Angulo: I don't know what it means.

Dr. Jung: In the case of the introvert his attitude toward his collective images is that of the extravert toward the outside world. He lives through them as in a romance or adventure. The extravert, on the other hand, takes his unconscious material in an introverted way, that is, with extreme caution and with many incantations to exorcise the inner power the object exercises over him. The extravert, seeing a

---

[1] This anecdote, as related, is not found in the literature.

green spot, jumps in and gets up to his neck in a swamp, but pulls out, shakes himself, and goes merrily on his way. If the introvert does that he is almost incapacitated for taking a walk ever again and blames everything in heaven and on the earth for his mistake. But if the swamp is in himself, he can jump in and come out unharmed, while to the extravert the swamp within himself is to be avoided at all costs.

LECTURE

You recall the dream I told you last time in which Siegfried was killed. In this dream something was fulfilled that had been suggested in the cave. The slain hero was there and here the murder is accomplished, so we can say of the dream that it is an elaboration of the vision in the cave. Of course, after such an event as the murder of the hero, things can be expected to happen. Siegfried stands for the ideal, and the killing of the ideal is the killing of the superior function, for it is the conquering function. A man with brains uses his intellect as his foremost tool, and this is truly an ideal; nor would he be adapted were this ideal not in harmony with other people's ideals of intellect. When the intellect or any superior function is pushed that far, it becomes bloodless and takes on an airy, gas-like character. Because it is a generally valid ideal, one thinks one has accomplished something very wonderful in differentiating a function to that extent, but in reality it is a very mechanical affair. Take an intellectual man and confront him with a woman who is a highly differentiated feeling type and there is a mutual disappointment, each finding the other empty and dry.

Impersonal feeling and thinking are very relativistic. When we look at them they seem something extraordinary, whereas in reality they are dead, because the personal unconscious is seeking to return to a more complete life away from the extreme differentiation of one function. So the primitive functions begin to increase. We cannot get anywhere in analysis with thinking until it reaches its antinomy—that is, something is and is not true at one and the same time. The same is true with feeling, and a differentiated feeling type must reach the point where the thing most loved is the thing most hated, before refuge will be sought in another function.

In the previous vision in the cave, the black scarab came after the fair-haired hero. The latter can be taken as the sun of the day, that is, the superior function. After he goes comes black night, which then

61

gives birth to a new sun. The thing that appears should be in our expectation a new hero, but in reality it is a midnight sun.

This idea of the sun of the day having its opposite in the night is an archetypal idea. Pythagoras, for example, thought that the earth had a twin. The idea also comes out in an anonymous book that was published during the war. This book was called *Peter Blobbs—Real Dreams*,[2] and the first dream, the one in which the midnight sun analogy appears, is called "The Night of the Swinging Censer." The dreamer is in an old cathedral which slowly fills with people. It is sunset time or after. In the middle of the cathedral there hangs a censer which is swinging to and fro. The more the night advances, the stronger grow the oscillations, and at the same time the church fills with hundreds of people clad in the costumes of all times and of all centuries. Finally even the primitives come in. As the church fills, the censer swings more and more and glows more brightly. At midnight the maximum is reached, and towards morning it decreases; with sunrise it comes to a standstill.

This is an extremely fine demonstration of the movement of the unconscious. As day fades the unconscious is activated, and by midnight the censer is in full blaze, but lighting up the past. As the dynamic principle increases in power, and the further back we go, the more are we overcome by the unconscious. Lunatics go furthest back to a strange psychological state where they cannot understand their ideas, nor are they able to make them understood by others. Sometimes, if it is in any way possible for a supposedly insane man to get his ideas understood, he can get well from the very strangest aberrations. Once a young Swiss man tried to jump into the carriage of the Empress of Germany with a bouquet of flowers. As he did so, he shouted out, "Les couleurs Suisses pour l'Impératrice!" His history was this: He was quite mad for a time and, identifying himself with Rousseau, went to the Isle Rousseau[3] and wrote a book of five thousand pages. While he was there on the Isle Rousseau, a German couple came there to live. The wife thought herself misunderstood and she and the young Swiss fell in love with each other. Then she could not stand him and fled to Berlin, being shortly followed by him. He had to look for her among the imperial family, for of course in no

---

[2] Not anonymous: Arthur John Hubbard, M.D., *Authentic Dreams of Peter Blobbs and of Certain of His Relatives* (London, 1916). The book was the subject of a seminar (apparently unrecorded) that Jung gave during the summer of 1920 in Cornwall, England. Cf. *Dream Analysis*, ed. William McGuire, introduction, p. ix.

[3] Probably the Île St-Pierre, in the Lake of Bienne, where J. J. Rousseau took refuge for two months in 1765.

lesser place was she to be found, and when he gave the bouquet to the Empress, it was to his mother-in-law to be.

I went very deeply into his analysis and found all his ideas to be in a perfectly logical sequence. He did not know why he should be considered insane, and he was certain that if the professors understood they would not lock him up. He has succeeded in making me understand him and finally I got his release. About two years ago I got a letter from him in America expressing his gratitude to me. He had married and was bringing up a family with success, and had had no return of his trouble. Because I had been able to follow him in his ideas, it was possible for him to work over from what to all intents and purposes seemed insanity, to reality. Later on I saw the same thing happen in other cases.

The more the dynamic principle gets into full swing, the greater is the power gained by the unconscious until the condition of dementia praecox may ensue. The dream of the censer showed very beautifully the slow advance of power as the night advanced. The flaming censer is analogous to the midnight sun, which becomes incandescent when the day sun, or superior function, goes out.

Why doesn't the inferior function come up at once? The inferior function is hooked up with the collective unconscious and has to come up first in the collective fantasies, which of course, in their first aspect, do not seem to be collective. One thinks of them as quite unique, and the people who have them are shy and withdrawn, and often suspicious, like people who hide a great secret. From this state to that of Godalmightiness is but a step. The person becomes more and more identical with the collective unconscious.

The next thing that happened to me was another fantastic vision. I used the same technique of the descent, but this time I went much deeper.[4] The first time I should say I reached a depth of about one thousand feet, but this time it was a cosmic depth. It was like going to the moon, or like the feeling of a descent into empty space. First the picture was of a crater, or a ring-chain of mountains, and my feeling association was that of one dead, as if oneself were a victim. It was the mood of the land of the hereafter.

I could see two people, an old man with a white beard and a young girl who was very beautiful. I assumed them to be real and listened to what they were saying. The old man said he was Elijah[5] and I was

---

[4] Cf. *MDR*, pp. 181f./174.

[5] *Transcript*: "Elias" (the German, as well as the Greek, form of Elijah). / For the figure of Salome, see below, Lectures 11 and 12.

quite shocked, but she was even more upsetting because she was Salome. I said to myself that there was a queer mixture: Salome and
Elijah, but Elijah assured me that he and Salome had been together
since eternity. This also upset me. With them was a black snake who
had an affinity for me. I stuck to Elijah as being the most reasonable
of the lot, for he seemed to have a mind. I was exceedingly doubtful
about Salome. We had a long conversation then but I did not understand it. Of course I thought of the fact of my father being a clergy-
man as being the explanation of my having figures like this. How
about this old man then? Salome was not to be touched upon. It was
only much later that I found her association with Elijah quite natural.
Whenever you take journeys like this you find a young girl with an
old man, and many examples of these two figures are to be found in
books familiar to you, such as those of Melville and Rider Haggard.[6]
In the Gnostic tradition it is said that Simon Magus always went about
with a young girl whom he had found in a brothel. She was named
Helen and was supposed to be a reincarnation of Helen of Troy.[7]
Then there are Kundry and Klingsor.[8] There is a book by a monk
of the fifteenth century, F. Colonna, 1450, called *Hypnerotomachia*
(Dream-love-conflict), in which the same story recurs.[9] Besides those
examples I have given of Haggard and Melville, there are the books
of Meyrink.[10]

[6] Cf. the theme of the priest and the maiden in Herman Melville's novel *Mardi*
(1849); for Rider Haggard's novel, *She*, see below, Lecture 15, n. 1, and end of Lecture
16.

[7] Cf. "Archetypes of the Collective Unconscious" (1934), CW 9 i, par. 64, and later
works. Jung had begun studying the Gnostic writers as early as 1910 (*MDR*, p. 162/
158) and, he has said, "seriously" from 1918 to the time of this seminar (ibid., pp.
200f./192f.).

[8] In Wagner's *Parsifal* (1882).

[9] Francesco Colonna, *Hypnerotomachia Poliphili* (Venice, 1499). Cf. the interpretive
study by a pupil of Jung's, Linda Fierz-David, *The Dream of Poliphilo* (tr. Mary Hottin-
ger, B.S., 1950; orig., Zurich, 1947).

[10] Gustav Meyrink, *Der Golem* (1915) and *Das grüne Gesicht* (1916), cited in *Types* (CW
6), par. 205, and in later works.

LECTURE 9

18 May 1925

(In a previous discussion[1] the point was made by Dr. Jung that the modern artist turns from the outer object to the inner, that is, to the images of the collective unconscious. In order to give examples of what he had said, Dr. Jung brought some photographs of the work of a sculptor who for a time had been a patient of his. Though it is difficult to give an account of the discussion of these pictures apart from the pictures themselves, so much of general application was said that it is worthwhile making the attempt.)

Dr. Jung: These sculptures are an effort on the part of the artist to express an experience of the collective unconscious. When one gets an intuition of the collective unconscious, if there is any creative power in the individual a definite figure is formed, rather than that the material comes through in a fragmentary form. It is true that it may come in this latter way, and usually does in dementia praecox, but if the creative faculty is there one tends to shape the material so that one could say that the normal form of contact with the collective unconscious is its appearance in the single form, and that when one is assailed by an inrush of fragmentary pictures, as in dementia praecox, there is disease.

When an artist has a figure from the collective unconscious, he at once begins to play with it esthetically, and usually makes some concretization of it as a monument, etc. This artist, as you see, had a love of the human figure and allowed his imagination to play around that. He got into his neurosis through the painting of a fresco, an order that came to him from a Protestant church. He was free to choose his own theme, and what he chose was the descent of the Holy Ghost at

[1] Lecture 7. The photographs discussed in the present lecture have not been found.

Pentecost. He began to make a composition and succeeded very well in grouping the apostles on either side, leaving the middle space open for the Holy Ghost. Then he could not make up his mind as to how he wanted to represent the Holy Ghost. He rejected the conventional symbol of the fire, and fell to speculating on what the Holy Ghost was like after all. While he was digging in his mind for the Holy Ghost, he stirred up the collective unconscious and then began to have wild nightmares and various other forms of terrors, so that by the time he came to me for treatment, he had forgotten all about his original quest of the Holy Ghost. While with me his task was to get the collective unconscious figures into plastic form.

As you noticed, the first figures are of gods with mouths open and dead eyes. The libido is being sucked back into the unconscious. Then he thought that these relatively simple things were inadequate, and so he began the figures that show the terrible complications. Finally he reduced these to an extraordinarily demoniacal figure closely paralleling one of the demon gods of Java. This then was the Holy Ghost to him. I later lost track of him.

Dr. Ward: Had he ever had anything which he called a religious experience?

Dr. Jung: Oh yes, these contacts with the collective unconscious were his religious experience and were understood by him in that sense. In this connection it is interesting to remember that Luther came to the conception of the dual aspect of God. He conceived of the manifest God and of the concealed God, the latter being a symbol of the evil forces of life. In other words, Luther was so impressed with the power of negative forces that it was necessary for him to preserve them to the deity; then the devil played only a secondary role between the two forces.

Mr. Aldrich: If this was the artist's negative conception of the deity, what was his positive conception? What were the figures he completed on the fresco?

Dr. Jung: These were more or less conventional representations of the apostles. Like all introverts, in his conscious he tended to remain academic.

(There were a number of written questions and the remainder of the hour was given over to them.)

Mrs. Evans' questions: "Is there not a pull or urge from each of the pairs of opposites that we have, and is that not necessary to preserve our balance? For instance: a person is both good and bad, generous and stingy, obstinate and yielding. Would the urge from only one of those opposites destroy him morally and physically?

"Are good and evil both necessary to the development of the individual personality? (*Psychology of the Unconscious* [1919 edn.], page 121.)

"In the middle, between the opposites, is there not inaction, a stationary condition without growth? Would that be the Nirvana so longed for by the Eastern mystic in his contemplation?"

Dr. Jung: This question, in order to be properly answered, involves a discussion of the pairs of opposites in a comprehensive way. Is it the wish of the class that we pause to do that now or postpone it for a later lecture?

(It was voted by the class to postpone the discussion of the pairs of opposites to a later meeting.)

Miss Corrie: In an earlier lecture you spoke of reversing the mental machinery in order to be a passive observer of dreams. In a later lecture[2] you say that watching the unconscious is only a perceptional connection and the worst possible attitude. I do not understand the distinction. Is it that you would have been adopting the night attitude by day?

Dr. Jung: The two lives do not belong together. When I said that I reversed the machinery in order to watch, I did not mean that it was merely for the purpose of watching. The purpose was the assimilation of my unconscious material, and the only way to achieve this is by giving the material a chance to come through. When one assumes a perceptional attitude toward one's unconscious, an attitude often to be observed in certain intuitives, one makes no effort to assimilate the material into the personality. There exists no moral relation then between the observed material and the personality. But if we observe in order to assimilate, it is an attitude that calls for the participation of all our functions. Nietzsche made the esthetical attitude the foremost attitude of man,[3] and the intellectual attitude can also be like this, that is, one can simply think about life without ever living. One is not in the process, not even one's own process. For the sake of consciousness we have had to step aside from life and observe; in other words, we have had to dissociate, but necessary as this process is in the evolution of consciousness, it ought not to be used as it is today as a means of keeping us out of life. Our effort today should be the double one of

[2] Cf. Lectures 4 and 6.
[3] Cf. *Types*, pars. 231–32.

consciousness plus a full participation in life. The common ideal of today is work at all costs, but many people simply work and do not live. We cannot depreciate the ideal of work, but we can understand that it is valueless when it divorces one from life.

Miss Henty's question: "Cannot the inferior functions be developed without such an overthrow of the superior functions as you described last time?"

Dr. Jung: Can you lift water up from the bottom of a falls without loss of energy? You have to have energy in order to activate the inferior function, and if you don't get this energy away from the superior function, whence is it to come? If you leave all your energy and will in the superior function you slowly go to hell—it sucks you dry. Normal people are those who can live under any circumstances without developing protests, but there are certain people in whom various conditions of life develop a protest. Take for example the effort to live a rounded life; it is most expensive. Today to bring up the inferior function is to live, but we pay dearly for it both in mistakes and in energy.

Sometimes it is not our choice—the inferior function takes us unawares. Such a situation presented itself at the time of the spread of Christianity two thousand years ago. The spiritual values had at that time sunk into the unconscious, and in order to realize them again, people had to go to tremendous lengths in the repudiation of material values. Gold, women, art—all had to be given up. Many even had to withdraw into the desert in order to free themselves from the world. Finally they came to the point of giving up life itself, and they were confronted with the arena and with being roasted alive. All this came to them through the growth of a psychological attitude. They were sacrificed because they undermined the most sacred ideals of the time. They threatened the disruption of the Roman family by their theological disputes. They refused to consider the Emperor divine. The effect they had on the collective viewpoint was similar to that produced today when anything is said against the god of Western Europe—Respectability. We today are also looking for certain other values. We seek life, not efficiency, and this seeking of ours is directly against the collective ideals of our times. Only those who have energy enough, or who have been gripped in spite of themselves, can go through this process, but once in it you have to bleed for it. It is a process that is going on all over the world today.

Mr. Robertson: What forced people into this attitude two thousand years ago?

Dr. Jung: People could see no other way of meeting the extreme to which paganism had led. The reversal of attitude which Christianity induced took the juice out of the literature and the art of the time. According to the philologists, everything of value disappeared then; only a faint flame remaining burning in Apuleius. But as a matter of fact, it was simply that the main stream of creative power left the channel dug by antiquity and sought a new bed. A new literature and art grew up, of which Tertullian is an example. The libido went over into spiritual values and an enormous change took place in human mentality in three hundred years. These collective movements are always hard for the individual to sustain. They grip people from the unconscious without their being able to know what has happened to them. Thus the literature of those days was full of a sickish sentimentality—the spark had gone from the conscious standpoint and was buried in the unconscious. These people in the early Christian era were unaware of the general movement contemporaneous with them. They could not realize they were Christians, yet they were seeking initiation into all sorts of mysteries in search of the thing Christianity was offering. They could not accept it because of its origin in the hands of despised peoples.

Most of the troubles of our times come from this lack of realization that we are part of a herd that has deviated from the main currents. When you are in a herd you lose the sense of danger, and this it is that makes us unable to see where we deviate from the deep currents of collectivity.

Miss Hincks: When you were speaking of bringing up your inferior function, did you mean the one in the unconscious?

Dr. Jung: Yes.

Miss Hincks: I understood you to mean that you had developed your intuition in contradistinction to your thinking.

Dr. Jung: No, I meant to place feeling in opposition to thinking. As a natural scientist, thinking and sensation were uppermost in me and intuition and feeling were in the unconscious and contaminated by the collective unconscious. You cannot get directly to the inferior function from the superior, it must always be via the auxiliary function. It is as though the unconscious were in such antagonism to the superior function that it allowed no direct attack. The process of working through the auxiliary functions goes on somewhat as follows: Suppose you have sensation strongly developed but are not fanatical about it. Then you can admit about every situation a certain aura of possibilities; that is to say, you permit an intuitive element to come in. Sensation as an auxiliary function would allow intuition to exist. But inasmuch as sensation (in the example) is a partisan of the intellect, intuition sides with the feeling, here the inferior function. Therefore the intellect will not agree with intuition, in this case, and will vote for its exclusion. Intellect will not hold together sensation and intuition, rather it will separate them. Such a destructive attempt will be checked by feeling, which backs up intuition.

Looking at it the other way around, if you are an intuitive type, you can't get to your sensations directly. They are full of monsters, and so you have to go by way of your intellect or feeling, whichever is the auxiliary in the conscious. It needs very cool reasoning for such a man to keep himself down to reality. To sum up then, the way is from the superior to the auxiliary, from the latter to the function opposite to the auxiliary. Usually this first conflict that is aroused between the auxiliary function in the conscious and its opposite function in the unconscious is the fight that takes place in analysis. This may be called the preliminary conflict. The knock-down battle between the superior and inferior functions only takes place in life. In the example of the intellectual sensation type, I suggested the preliminary conflict would be between sensation and intuition, and the final fight between intellect and feeling.

Dr. de Angulo: Why cannot the main battle take place in analysis?

Dr. Jung: That can only happen when the analyst loses his objectivity and becomes personally involved with the patient. In this connection it can be said that the analyst is always in danger of intoxications through his unconscious. Suppose a woman comes and tells me I am her savior. While consciously I may know perfectly well she has made a terrible projection upon me, unconsciously I drink it up and possibly swell to tremendous proportions.

Mrs. Keller's question: (This question as originally presented was lost. The problem concerned was in connection with the will.)

Dr. Jung: It cannot be said that the will of man is like a stone rolling downhill. What is true is that through the will you can release a process, say a fantasy, which then proceeds on its own course. There are two ways of looking at will. That of Schopenhauer, for instance, who speaks of the will to live and the will to death in the sense of an urge to life and an urge to death. I like to reserve the concept of will for that small amount of energy that is disposable by us in consciousness. Now if you put this small amount toward activating the instinctive process, the latter then goes on with a force much bigger than yours.

The libido of man contains the two opposite urges or instincts: the instinct to live and the instinct to die. In youth the instinct toward life is stronger, and that is why young people don't cling to life—they have it. The libido as an energetic phenomenon contains the pairs of opposites, otherwise there would be no movement of the libido. It is a metaphor to use the terms of life and death; any others will do, so long as they show the opposition. In animals and in primitive peoples, the pairs of opposites are closer together than in so-called civilized peoples, hence both animals and primitives part with life more easily than do we. A primitive can kill himself just for the luxury of haunting an enemy. In other words, because of our dissociation, the pairs of opposites are much further apart. This gives us our increased psychical energy, and the price we pay is one-sidedness.

nevrosis

When the pairs of opposites are close together, the individual changes easily. He passes quickly from a mood of expansion to a mood of death.

We have now come into a discussion of the pairs of opposites. Is it the wish of the class to discuss this problem at the next meeting?

(It was so voted by the class.)

LECTURE 10

25 May 1925

Dr. Jung:

Is there any particular way you would like to approach the problem of the pairs of opposites?

Dr. de Angulo: I would like to begin with them as they appear in nature and work up to them as they appear in man.

Dr. Jung: That would be beginning at the roof inasmuch as, in a certain sense, the notion of the pairs of opposites is a projection upon nature. For that reason it is better for us to begin with our psychological experience of the pairs of opposites, for we are not at all sure of the objectivity of the world. Thus, for example, there is the widespread theory of monism, which is a denial of the dualistic aspect of the world—that is, it insists on our oneness and the world's oneness. If you hold the theory of the pairs of opposites, you can hold both monism and dualism which will then become a pair of opposites, but here you will find yourself once more in the magic circle of your own personality. You cannot get out of your skin until you become an eternal ghost.

There is a written question from Miss Hincks which takes us into the philosophical aspect of the problem, from which side I think we will find the best approach.

Miss Hincks' question: "In treating the opposites in analysis, do you consider them as psychological, or as biological phenomena from which the elements of opposition can be removed, in contradistinction to the philosophical viewpoint where they are qualities logically opposed and therefore irreconcilable?"

Dr. Jung: The idea of the pairs of opposites is as old as the world, and if we treated it properly, we should have to go back to the earliest sources of Chinese philosophy, that is to the *I Ching*[1] oracle. Curi-

---

[1] *Transcript: "Yi King."* So spelled in the translation by James Legge (Sacred Books of the East, XVI, 2nd ed., Oxford, 1899), the only version available in English in 1925.

ously enough, the pairs of opposites do not appear as such in Egyptian thought, but they are a basic part of both Chinese and Indian philosophy. In the *I Ching*, they appear as an ever-recurring enantiodromia, through the action of which one state of mind leads inevitably to its opposite. This is the essential idea of Taoism, and the writings of both Lao-tse and Confucius are permeated with this principle.

We have the *I Ching*, the source of Chinese philosophy, in the form given it by King Wên and the Duke Chou, who employed a prison term, so it is said, in working out an intuitive interpretation of the *I Ching* oracle. Some of you know the technique of the *I Ching*. The arrangement is in the form of hexagrams symbolizing the enantiodromia to be expressed. It might be called a contradiction psychology, that is, while the *a* principle is increasing, its opposite the *b* principle is decreasing, but there always comes a point where *b* imperceptibly begins increasing until it is the dominant. This same conception is involved in the symbol of Tao, where the opposing principles are represented by white and black spiral divisions of a circle. They are thought of as the male and female elements respectively. The white portion, or masculine principle, contains within it a black spot, and the black portion, or female principle, contains a white spot. Thus Yang the masculine principle, when at its full, generates Yin the feminine, and vice versa.

The *Tao Tê Ching* is also founded on these principles of the opposites, though expressed in a somewhat different way. It is possible that the author of the *Tao Tê Ching*, Lao-tse, was in some way in connection with the philosophy of the *Upanishads*, as there is a similarity between the two. Perhaps among the books of the king whom he served as librarian there were to be found Brahmanic texts, or perhaps the contact was made through travellers. In Lao-tse the idea of the opposites is expressed in this way: High rests upon Low, Great Good and Great Evil, that is to say, nothing exists save by virtue of a balancing opposite. It is the same notion Nietzsche voices when he says the greater the spread of the tree, the deeper the roots.

(Jung's library contained all but four of the 50 vols. of the Sacred Books of the East.) References herein are given to *The I Ching or Book of Changes*, the Richard Wilhelm translation rendered into English by Cary F. Baynes, with Jung's foreword (New York/Princeton and London, 1950; 3rd ed., 1967. The foreword is also in CW 11). The English translator was formerly Dr. de Angulo, recorder of the present seminar. Jung's interest in the *I Ching* dated from around 1920 (*MDR*, p. 373/342); he and Wilhelm first met around 1923.

The philosophical position of India with respect to the opposites is more advanced. There the teaching is, "Be free of the pairs of opposites, don't pay attention to High and Low." The perfect man must be above his virtues as well as above his vices. It is again the same idea that Nietzsche expresses when he says, "Master your virtues as well as your vices." So in the *Upanishads*, in contrast to the Chinese viewpoint, the emphasis is not on the opposites as such, but on the peculiar creative process between them. One could say therefore that the general point of view of the *Upanishads* is monistic. Atman is the central thing between the opposites; they themselves are almost taken for granted. Lao-tse on the other hand, as we have seen, stresses the opposites, although he knows the way between the two, Tao, and accepts it as the essence of life. Still he is always concerned with the pedagogic aspect of the problem; it is his intention that his pupils never are to forget that they are in the way of oppositions, and he has to teach them the things that will lead them along that way.

The Brahman pupil, on the other hand, does not have to be taught these things; he knows them. Perhaps this grows out of the fact, in the case of the Brahman, [that] it is a matter of the wisdom having been handed down through the caste. The knowledge of the opposites was a possession of this priestly caste and did not need to be taught. The Brahman pupil, in a word, stood on a certain philosophical *niveau* by virtue of his birth and was ready for the next step, namely the thing between the pairs of opposites, whereas the people whom Lao-tse addressed were on no such aristocratic level, spiritually speaking; they were the people of average intelligence. The legend about Lao-tse's writing down his wisdom before his retirement into solitude is an example of what I mean. Lao-tse is said to have left his home on the slope of the mountain and to have wandered west. When he reached the gate in the Great Wall, the guard recognized him at once and would not let him pass through the gate until he had written down his wisdom. He wrote it then in the book of five thousand words, the *Tao Tê Ching*. This legend would show that the book was meant for the generally learned, not just for a priest class. The *Upanishads* appeal to people who are beyond the pairs of opposites. If you are free of illusion, life is worthwhile and not worthwhile to an almost equal degree, but such people could only be frequent in a class specially devoted to philosophical training.

In those times, what philosophers thought was nature itself. It was not very intentional; rather, thought happened to people in a strangely direct and immediate way so as to give the impression of being given to the mind rather than made by it. Of course, innumerable examples of this sort of thing occur to us if we begin to think of great discoveries and works of art. Mayer's conception of energy came this way, as though from heaven.[2] So also the *Devil's Sonata* of Tartini.[3] Raphael's *Madonna* (now in Dresden) was the result of a sudden vision, as was Michelangelo's *Moses*.[4] When a thought or a vision comes to a man in this way, it is with an overwhelming power of conviction. This, as I say, is the type of original thought. Today we have lost to a great extent this sense of the immanence of thought, as one might put it, and have instead the illusion of making our thoughts ourselves. We are not convinced that our thoughts are original beings that walk about in our brains, and we invent the idea that they are powerless without our gracious creative act; we invent this in order not to be too much influenced by our thoughts. We are in relation to our thoughts a little bit like Chanteclair with the sun: convinced that the sun could not rise without his crowing, he was persuaded once to make the experiment, but just as the sun came up, so great was his mistrust of its powers, that he crowed, making sure thereby, that the world would not be without the sun that day.

Of course it is quite useful to us to have the idea that our thoughts are free expressions of our intentional thinking, otherwise we would never be free from the magic circle of nature. After all, we really can think, even if not with an absolute independence from nature; but it is the duty of the psychologist to make the double statement, and while admitting man's power of thought, to insist also on the fact that he is trapped in his own skin, and therefore always has his thinking influenced by nature in a way he cannot wholly control.

As I said, this original thinking is immediately convincing. When you have such a thought, you are sure it is true—it comes as a revelation. This is no more beautifully shown than in a projection; you simply know it to be true, and you are inclined to resent any suggestion of error connected with it. This is especially true with women,

---

[2] Julius Robert Mayer, German physicist, in the 1840s. Cf. "On the Psychology of the Unconscious" (1917), CW 7, pars. 106ff.

[3] Giuseppe Tartini, Italian violinist and composer, 18th cent. For his inspirational dream, see *Encyclopaedia Britannica*, 11th ed., s.v. Tartini.

[4] The *Sistine Madonna*, in the Gemäldegalerie, Dresden; the *Moses* in San Pietro in Vincoli, Rome. According to a historian of the art of the Italian Renaissance, John Shearman, the early literature offers no evidence that these works were inspired by visions. Shearman suggests that Jung's statement is a "reification of some loose talk in 19th-century monographs. . . . The odd thing is that each work of art *represents* a vision."

where the projection may not even be conscious. The unconscious has power to influence our thinking in incredible ways. Thus I remember once reading a passage in one of Lamprecht's books[5] to the effect that it is quite evident that man has passed through an age of incest. I accepted this as I read it, but then I said to myself, "Why is it evident that man has passed through an age of incest?"—and the more I thought of it, the less evident it became. Lamprecht was no doubt guided in his assumption by the unconscious acceptance of the Adam and Eve myth. So there is a certain kind of thinking gripping us all the time, and these unconscious ideas act as the players of marionettes.

Insofar as natural thinking carried with it the conviction of natural fact, the early philosophers when thinking about nature had some such sudden revelation, as we would say, come to them, and they took it for granted that nature herself had spoken to them and that they were in possession of a truth of nature, indisputably true. It never occurred to them that it might be a projection, and without foundation in the world of fact. Thus it was with the principle of the opposites; it was held by the early philosophers to have been given to man by nature. The legend says of the *I Ching* that a horse came up out of the Yellow River bearing on his back the trigrams out of which the symbols are built up. The sages copied it and it was known as the River Map.[6]

We do not think thus, and so we no longer take our thoughts as nature; the very way thought processes work in us keeps us from the notion that nature has spoken to us when we have thought. But these people allowed their minds to work without control, and inasmuch as the brain is also a phenomenon of nature, it is a true product of nature and therefore contains the result of the action of the forces of nature. The fruit of the brain is a natural product and as such must be assumed to contain the general principles of nature. A very wise man could construct the whole world from one apple. He could tell you the climate that made it possible, the tree that bore it, the animals that eat it, in short everything about it, for all is related to all. Why then should it not be supposed that the brain could produce a perfectly natural fruit which would reproduce all nature? Obviously there is no law to prove that this is so, but we cannot assume that the products of our brains do not derive from nature; therefore I see no

[5] Karl Lamprecht, German crank historian. Cf. *Dream Analysis*, p. 192.
[6] Usually called the Yellow River Map. Cf. the *I Ching*, 3rd ed., pp. 309, 320.

reason why we would not find astonishingly true things in the thought of the ancient sages, such as the *I Ching* represents. Confucius is said to have regretted not having spent his whole life in the study of the *I Ching*, and to have said that it only failed him once as a guide in his actions.

Since the earliest times, then, the pairs of opposites have been the theme of men's thoughts. The next important philosopher we have to consider in connection with them is Heraclitus. He is singularly Chinese in his philosophy and is the only Western man who has ever really compassed the East. If the Western world had followed his lead, we would all be Chinese in our viewpoint instead of Christian. We can think of Heraclitus as making the switch between East and West. After him, the next person in history to become deeply and seriously concerned with the problem of the pairs of opposites is Abelard, but he has stripped off all connection with nature and has intellectualized the problem entirely.

The most recent resurrection of the problem is through analysis. Freud has a great deal to say about the pairs of opposites as they present themselves in pathological psychology. In a case of sadism, masochism is always to be found in the unconscious, and vice versa. A man who is a miser on one side is a spendthrift on the other. We all know the cruelty possible in excessively good people, and that respectable people are so often blessed with hellions as sons.[7] In the works of both Freud and Adler there is a continuous play of this principle of above and below.

I also approached the problem from the pathological side, first in sexual psychology, and then with respect to the character as a whole. I formulated it as a heuristic principle always to seek for the opposite of every given trend, and all along the line the principle worked. Extreme fanaticism I found to rest on a concealed doubt. Torquemado, as the father of the Inquisition, was as he was because of the insecurity of his faith; that is, he was unconsciously as full of doubt as he was consciously full of faith. So in general any excessively strong position brings forth its opposite. I traced this phenomenon down to the fundamental split in the libido, by virtue of which split we can never crave anything violently without at the same time destroying it. A very vivid example of this took place with a patient of mine. She was a young woman who was engaged to a man whom she could not marry because of financial hardships. Finally he went away to Japan

[7] *Transcript*: "hells of sons." Garbled?

and stayed three years. She wrote him the most beautiful love letters all during this time and could scarcely live from day to day so great was her yearning for him. Then he sent for her and they were married. Almost immediately she became completely insane and had to be sent home.

So when you say "Yes" you say at the same time "No." This principle may seem a hard one, but as a matter of fact there must be this split in the libido or nothing works and we remain inert.[8] Life is never so beautiful as when surrounded by death. Once I had a very wealthy patient who on coming to me said, "I don't know what you are going to do with me, but I hope you are going to give me something that isn't grey." And that is exactly what life would be if there were no opposites in it; therefore the pairs of opposites are not to be understood as mistakes but as the origin of life. For the same thing holds in nature. If there is no difference in high and low, no water can come down. Modern physics expresses the condition that would ensue were the opposites removed from nature by the term entropy: that is, death in an equable tepidity. If you have all your wishes fulfilled, you have what could be called psychological entropy. I found, then, that what I had thought to be a pathological phenomenon is in fact a rule of nature. We are part of the general energic process, and it is psychology looked at with this fact in mind that I have tried to present in the *Types*.

When I was beginning *Types*, I had a letter from a French editor who wanted me to contribute a book in a series he was arranging on oppositions. He sent me a long list of these opposites to consider: action and inaction, spirituality and materialism, etc., but I avoided all these derived or subordinate oppositions and occupied myself with tracing them down to something fundamental. I started with the primitive idea of the flowing out and the flowing in of energy, and from this I constructed the theory of the introverted and extraverted types.[9]

As you remember from a previous lecture, I had come upon this notion of a split in the libido at the time I was working on the *Psychology of the Unconscious*, but the phrase "split in the libido" could lead to a misconception. The libido is not split in itself; it is a case of a balancing movement between opposites, and you could say that libido

---

[8] This and the preceding sentence are quoted in Joan Corrie, *ABC of Jung's Psychology* (London, 1928), p. 58.

[9] "A Contribution to the Study of Psychological Types" (CW 6), pars. 499ff., originally a lecture in German, revised in a French version, both 1913.

is one or that libido is two according as you concentrate now on the flow, now on the opposing poles between which the flow takes place. The opposition is a necessary condition of libido flow,[10] and so you may say that by virtue of that fact one is committed to a dualistic conception of the world; but you can also say that the "flow"—that is, the energy—is one, and that is monism. If there is no high and low, no water flows; if there is high and low and no water, nothing happens; thus there is at the same time duality and oneness in the world, and it is a matter of temperament which viewpoint you choose to assume. If you are a dualist like Lao-tse, and concerned chiefly with the opposites, all you will find to say about what is between might go into his words, "Tao is so still." But if, on the other hand, you are monistic like the Brahmans, you can write whole volumes about Atman, the thing between the opposites.

Thus monism and dualism are psychological problems without intrinsic validity. What we are more nearly concerned with is the existence of the pairs of opposites. To us, in a way, it is a new discovery that all things are in opposition; we are still reluctant to accept the bad of our good, and the fact that our ideals are based on things far from ideal. We have to learn with effort the negations of our positions, and to grasp the fact that life is a process that takes place between two poles, being only complete when surrounded by death. We are really in the position of Lao-tse's pupils and need to say of the Tao, "It is so still," for it is not loud to us. But when we become aware of the opposites we are driven to seek the way that will resolve them for us, for we cannot live in a world that is and is not, we must go forward to a creation that enables us to attain a third point superior to the pairs of opposites. We could adopt Tao and Atman as our solutions, possibly, but only on the assumption that these terms have meant to their originators what our philosophical ideas mean to us. But that is not so; Tao and Atman grew, Atman out of the lotus, while Tao is the still water. That is to say, they were revelations, while to us they are concepts and leave us cold. We cannot assimilate them as did the men in those days. To be sure, the theosophists attempt it, with the result, however, of going up in the air like so many windbags, and with all connections with reality severed.

These revelations happened to those people, they grew out of them just as the apple grows from the tree. For us, they give great satisfaction to the intellect, but for uniting the pairs of opposites they serve

[10] The preceding sentence and this one, to here, are quoted in Corrie, *ABC*, p. 58.

nothing. Suppose a patient comes to me with a great conflict and I say to him, "Read the *Tao Tê Ching*" or "Throw your sorrows on Christ." It is splendid advice, but what does it mean to the patient in helping his conflict? Nothing. To be sure, the thing for which Christ stands does work for Catholics and partly for Protestants, but it does not work for everybody; and nearly all my patients are people for whom the traditional symbols do not work. So our way has to be one where the creative character is present, where there is a process of growth which has the quality of revelation. Analysis should release an experience that grips us or falls upon us as from above, an experience that has substance and body, such as those things occurred to the ancients. If I were going to symbolize it I would choose the Annunciation.

Swedenborg had an experience of this immediate and challenging character. He was in London at an inn, and after having had a very good dinner, later in the evening he suddenly saw the whole floor covered with snakes and toads. He was greatly frightened, and still more so when there appeared before him a man in a red mantle. You imagine, no doubt, that this apparition spoke weighty words to Swedenborg, but what he said was, "Don't eat so much!" Thus did Swedenborg's thought take on bodily form, and because of being so objective, it had a tremendous effect on him. He was shaken to the depths by it.[11]

Another similar case comes to my mind, that of a man who drank. One evening he came home after a very fine carouse, dead drunk. He heard people upstairs having a great feast, and that he enjoyed. At five o'clock he went to the window to see what the great noise was. He lived in an alley with some sycamore trees outside his window. There he saw a cattle fair in progress, but with all the pigs in the trees. He raised a great shout to call attention to them, and then the police took him to the insane asylum. When he came to a realization of what had happened to him, he had finished with drinking.

In both these cases, nature produced a great terror, and though the examples are grotesque, nonetheless they illustrate the point I was making to the effect that the representation that liberates must have an ancient character, then it is convincing. It must be organically true, that is, in and of our own being. We know there is no method by which we can force these events, but the world is full of methods

[11] Cf. Jung's foreword to Suzuki's *Introduction to Zen Buddhism* (1939; CW 11), par. 882, where the anecdote is told differently.

to produce states of mind that facilitate contact with immediate truth. Of these methods, yoga is the most conspicuous example. There are several different kinds of yoga, those that have to do with breathing, exercises, fasting, etc., and again others such as Kundalini yoga,[12] which is a sort of sexual training somewhat obscene in character. Sexuality is taken because it is an instinctive condition and therefore liable to induce states in which these immediate experiences can take place. All these yoga methods, and practices similar to them, will bring about the desired condition, but only if God be willing, so to speak; that is to say, there is another factor involved which is necessary, but the nature of which we do not know. All kinds of primitive practices are to be understood as an effort on the part of man to make himself receptive to a revelation from nature.

[12] This is the earliest reference to Kundalini yoga in Jung's recorded work. In the autumn of 1932, Jung and a German Indologist, J. W. Hauer, gave a seminar, mostly in English, on this subject. Cf. *General Bibliography* (CW 19), p. 211, 1932a.

LECTURE 11

1 June 1925

Dr. Jung:
There were questions left over from the previous meeting, and as I have forgotten to bring them with me this time I will ask that they be put verbally now. Mrs. Keller, you had something, I believe.

Mrs. Keller: I would like to know something more about the ancestral image and the way it affects the life of the individual.

Dr. Jung: I am afraid I have not enough experience to elucidate such a question. My ideas on the subject are after all rather tentative, but I can give you an example of how the thing seems to me to work. Suppose a man to have had a normal development for some forty years or so, then he comes into a situation which awakens an ancestral complex. The complex will be awakened because the situation is one in which the individual is best adapted through this ancestral attitude. Let us say that this imaginary normal man we are talking about gets into a responsible position where he wields much power. He himself was never made to be a leader, but among his inherited units there is the figure of such a leader, or the possibility of it. That unit now takes possession of him, and from that time on he has a different character. God knows what has become of him, it is really as though he had lost himself and the ancestral unit had taken over and devoured him. His friends can't make out what has happened to him, but there he is, a different person from what he was before. There may not even be a conflict developed within him, though that frequently comes; it may be that the image has just so much vitality that the ego recedes before it and yields to its domination.

Mrs. Keller: But if the image is demanded in order for him to fill that place, how can he come to peace with himself and at the same time conquer the image in case of conflict?

Dr. Jung: Well, in general the only thing to do is to attempt by analytical treatment to reconcile these images with the ego. If the person is weak, then the image takes possession. One sees this happening over and over again with girls when they marry. They may have been perfectly normal girls up to that time, and then up comes some role they feel called upon to play—the girl is no longer herself. The usual result is a neurosis. I recall the case of a mother with four children who complained that never had she had any important experiences in life. "What about your four children?" I asked her. "Oh," she said, "they just happened to me." One could almost say that her grandmother and not herself had had those children, and as a matter of fact, she did repudiate them.

Are there not more questions? Dr. Mann?

Dr. Mann: I handed in a question which I think will probably be answered in the further course of the lectures. I wanted to know if you would trace the progress of an irrational type from the superior to the inferior function as you traced it for us in the rational type through your own experience.

Dr. Jung: Take then an intuitive type whose auxiliary function is thinking, and suppose him to have reached the top of intuition and to have failed there. As you know, the intuitive is always rushing after new possibilities. Finally he gets himself, let us suppose, into a hole and can't get out. There is nothing he so dreads as just this—he abominates permanent attachments and prisons, but here he is in a hole at last, and he sees no way that his intuition can get him out. There is a river passing, and railroad trains go by, but he is left just where he is—stuck. Now then perhaps he begins to *think* what could be done. When he takes up his intellectual function, he is likely to come into conflict with his feeling, for through his thinking he will seek devious ways out of his difficulty, a lie here, or some cheating there, which will not be acceptable to his feeling. He must then choose between his feeling and his intellect, and in making this choice he comes to a realization of the gap that exists between the two. He will get out of this conflict by discovering a new kingdom, namely that of sensation, and then for the first time reality takes on a new meaning for him. To an intuitive type who has not brought up his sensation, the world of the sensation type looks very like a lunar landscape—that is, empty and dead. He thinks the sensation type spends his life with corpses, but once he has taken up this inferior function in himself, he begins to enjoy the object as it really is and for its own sake instead of seeing it through an atmosphere of his projections.

People with an overdevelopment of intuition which leads them to scorn objective reality, and so finally to a conflict such as I have described above, have usually characteristic dreams. I once had as a patient a girl of the most extraordinary intuitive powers, and she had pushed the thing to such a point that her own body even was unreal to her. Once I asked her half jokingly if she had never noticed that she had a body, and she answered quite seriously that she had not—she bathed herself under a sheet! When she came to me she had ceased even to hear her steps when she walked—she was just floating through the world. Her first dream was that she was sitting on top of a balloon, not even in a balloon, if you please, but on top of one that was high up in the air, and she was leaning over peeping down at me. I had a gun and was shooting at the balloon which I finally brought down. Before she came to me she had been living in a house where she had been impressed with the charming girls. It was a brothel and she had been quite unaware of the fact. This shock brought her to analysis.

I cannot bring such a case down to a sense of reality through sensation directly, for to the intuitive, facts are mere air; so then, since thinking is her auxiliary function, I begin to reason with her in a very simple way till she becomes willing to strip from the fact the atmosphere she has projected upon it. Suppose I say to her, "Here is a green monkey." Immediately she will say, "No, it is red." Then I say, "A thousand people say this monkey is green, and if you make it red, it is only of your own imagination." The next step is to get her to the point where her feeling and thinking conflict. An intuitive does with her feelings very much the same thing she does with her thoughts; that is, if she gets a negative intuition about a person, then the person seems all evil, and what he really is matters not at all. But little by little such a patient begins to ask what the object is like after all, and to have the desire to experience the object directly. Then she is able to give sensation its proper value, and she stops looking at the object from around a corner; in a word, she is ready to sacrifice her overpowering desire to master by intuition.

To a sensation type what I have said about the workings of the mind of an intuitive will doubtless seem utter nonsense, so different are the ways in which the two types see reality. I had once a patient who after about six months of analysis with me awoke with a sort of shock to the fact that I did not have large blue eyes. Another, having a still longer acquaintanceship with my study, which is painted green, asked me why I had changed it from the oak paneling that had been there all the time she had been coming to me. Only with the greatest difficulty could I persuade her that she it was who paneled the room in oak.

The same falsification of reality is the characteristic of all superior functions when they are pushed to the limit of development. The purer they become, the more do they try to force reality into a scheme. The world has all four functions in it—perhaps more, and it is not possible to keep in touch with it if one disregards one or more of the functions.

Miss Corrie's question: "Will you please explain the relation of ambivalence to the pairs of opposites?"

Dr. Jung: If you take the pairs of opposites you are almost supposing two parties at war with one another—this is a dualistic conception. Ambivalence is a monistic conception; there the opposites do not appear as split apart, but as contrasting aspects of one and the same thing. Take for instance a man who has good and bad sides—such a man is ambivalent. We say about him that he is weak, that he is torn between God and the Devil—all the good is in God, all the bad in the Devil; and he is an atom swaying between the two, and you can never tell what he is going to do; his character has never established itself, but remains ambivalent. On the other hand, we can have a son who stands in between conflicting parents—nothing said of his character, he is the victim of these opposites; and so he can remain indefinitely. One had to invent the term "image" to meet this situation. Such a person can make no progress until he realizes that he has only stated half the case when he thinks himself victimized between the pairs of opposites, father and mother. He must know that he carries the images of the two within himself, and that within his own mind such a conflict is going on—in other words, that he is ambivalent. Until he comes to this realization, he can use the actual parents or their images as weapons with which to protect himself against meeting life. If he admits that the conflicting parties are parts of himself, he assumes responsibility for the problem they represent. In the same way I can see no sense in our blaming the war for things that have happened to us. Each of us carried within himself the elements that brought on the war.

The connection between ambivalence and the pairs of opposites is, then, a subjective standpoint.

Mr. Robertson: If the libido is conceived of as split always, where is the thing that gives the push in one direction or another?

Dr. Jung: The question of a push does not enter in, because libido, energy, is by hypothesis in movement. The expression "ambitendency" is a way of denominating the contradictory nature of energy. There is no potential without opposites, and therefore one has ambitendency. The substance of energy so to speak is a dissipation of energy, that is, one never observes energy save as having movement and in a direction. A mechanical process is theoretically reversible, but in nature energy always moves in one direction, that is, from a higher to a lower level. So in the libido it has also direction, and it can be said of any function that it has a purposive nature. Of course, the well-known prejudice against this viewpoint that has existed in biology has to do with the confusion of teleology with purpose. Teleology says there is an aim toward which everything is tending, but such an aim could not exist without presupposing a mind that is leading us to a definite goal, an untenable viewpoint for us. However, processes can show purposive character without having to do with a preconceived goal, and all biological processes are purposive. The essence of the nervous system is purposive since it acts like a central telegraph office for coordinating all parts of the body. All the suitable nervous reflexes are gathered in the brain. Coming back to the original point about the ambitendency, energy is not split in itself, it is the pairs of opposites and also undivided—in other words, it presents a paradox.

Mr. Robertson: It is not clear to me how you distinguish between teleological and purposeful.

Dr. Jung: There can be a purposive character to an action without the anticipation of a goal. This idea is fully developed in Bergson, as you know. I can very well go in a direction without having in mind the final goal. I can go toward a pole without having the idea of going to it. I use it for orientation but not for a goal. One speaks of the blindness of instinct, but nonetheless instinct is purposive. It works properly only under certain conditions, and as soon as it gets out of tune with these conditions it threatens the destruction of the species. The old war instinct of primitive man applied to modern nations, with their inventions of gassing, etc., becomes suicidal.

Mr. Robertson's written question: "You have presented the two views that are held by the psychological types—the introvert looks at the top and the bottom of the waterfall, while the extravert looks at the water in between.

"But are not you yourself looking 'at the top and bottom' in formulating the idea above? Thus you have illustrated your own tendency (introvertive) to see enantiodromia. Or would you claim some *objective* validity to this particular concept?"

Dr. Jung: Certainly seeing the top and the bottom is an introverted attitude, but that is just the place the introvert fills. He has distance between himself and the object and so is sensitive to types—he can separate and discriminate. He does not want too many facts and ideas about. The extravert is always calling for facts and more facts. He usually has one great idea, a fat idea you might say, that will stand for a unity back of all these facts, but the introvert wants to split that very fat idea.

When it comes to a matter of objective validity, one can say that since so many people see this enantiodromia there must be truth in it, and since so many people see a continuous development, there must be truth in that too, but strictly speaking objective validity cannot be claimed, only subjective. Of course this is not very satisfactory, and the introvert is always having the tendency to say privately that his viewpoint is the only correct one, subjectively taken.

Dr. de Angulo: I don't see the logical connection between introversion and the ability to see the phenomenon of enantiodromia. There must be millions of extraverts who see that too.

Dr. Jung: There is no logical connection, but I have observed it to be a temperamental difference between the two attitudes. Introverts want to see little things grow big and big things grow little. Extraverts like great things—they do not want to see good things going into worse, but always into better. An extravert hates to think of himself as containing a hellish opposite. Moreover, the introvert leans toward accepting enantiodromia easily, because such a concept robs the object of much power, while the extravert, having no desire to minimize the importance of the object, is willing to credit it with power.

Mr. Aldrich: It seems to me, Dr. Jung, that some of what you have said is in contradiction to what you say in *Types* about the extraverted nominalist holding facts discretely, and the introverted realist seeking always unity through abstraction.[1]

Dr. Jung: No, there is no contradiction there. The nominalist, though he has his emphasis on discrete facts, creates a sort of compensated unity by imagining an eternal Being who covers them all. The realist is wanting not so much to get to a unit idea as to get away from the facts to an abstraction of them in ideas. Goethe's idea of the "Urpflanze"[2] is an example of an idea that is too general, and illustrates what I mean by the tendency of extraverts to formulate "great

---

[1] Cf. CW 6, pars. 40ff.

[2] Cf. Goethe, *Versuch die Metamorphose der Pflanzen zu erklären* (1790).

ideas." Agassiz,[3] on the other hand, developed the notion that animal beings came from separate types, and this fits the introvert much better than Goethe's conception. In a Platonist's idea of life, there is always a limited number of primordial images, but still there are many, not just one—so the introvert has the tendency to be polytheistic.

Mr. Aldrich: But did not Plato ascribe the origin of the world to the mind of God?

Dr. Jung: Yes, he did, but all the interest in Plato is not on this conception, but on the conception of the *eidola,* or primordial abstract ideas.[4]

LECTURE

I told you last time[5] about the dream concerning the killing of the hero and then the fantasy about Elijah and Salome.

Now the killing of the hero is not an indifferent fact, but one that involves typical consequences. Dissolving an image means that you become that image. Doing away with the concept of God means that you become that God. This is so because if you dissolve an image it is always consciously, and then the libido invested in the image goes into the unconscious. The stronger the image the more you are caught by it in the unconscious, so if you give up the hero in the conscious you are forced into the hero role by the unconscious.

I remember a case in point in this connection. This was a man who was able to give me a very excellent analysis of his situation. His mother had repeatedly told him, as he was growing up, that he would some day be a savior of mankind, and though he did not quite believe it, still it got him in a certain way, and he began to study and finally went to the university. There he broke down and went home. But a savior does not have to study chemistry, and moreover a savior is always misunderstood, and so nursed along in these ideas by his mother and by his own fantasy, he allowed himself to slump completely on his conscious side. He was content to take a position in an insurance company which amounted to little more than licking stamps. All the time he was playing the secret role of the despised of

---

[3] Louis Agassiz, Swiss-American natural scientist, who held a theory of "multiple creation." Jung cited him nowhere else, though his library contains a copy of Agassiz's *Schöpfungsplan* (1875).

[4] Cf., e.g., *Timaeus* 37d.

[5] Actually in Lecture 8, at n. 5.

men. Finally he came to me. When I analyzed him I found this fantasy of the savior. He had understood it only intellectually, and so the emotional grip it had had on him remained unchanged—in spite of all he thought about it, he was still drawing satisfaction out of being an unrecognized savior.

It seemed as though the analysis would arouse him sufficiently, but even that did not sink in. He thought it was very interesting to live in such an odd fantasy. Then he began to do better in his work, and later applied for and won a directorship in a large factory. Here he collapsed utterly. He could not see that he had not realized the emotional value of the fantasy, and that it was the operation of these unrealized emotional values that had made him apply for a position he was in no way fitted to fill. His fantasy was really nothing but a power fantasy, and his desire to be a savior was based on a power motive. One can thus come to a realization of such a fantasy system, and yet have its activity persist in the unconscious.

The killing of the hero, then, means that one is made into a hero and something hero-like must happen.

Besides Elijah and Salome, there was a third factor in the fantasy I began to describe, and that is the huge black snake between them. The snake indicates the counterpart of the hero. Mythology is full of this relationship between the hero and the snake.[6] A northern myth says the hero has eyes of a snake, and many myths show the hero being worshipped as a snake, having been transformed into it after death. This is perhaps from the primitive idea that the first animal that creeps out of the grave is the soul of the man who was buried.

The presence of the snake then says it will be again a hero myth. As to the meaning of the two figures, Salome is an anima figure, blind because, though connecting the conscious and the unconscious, she does not see the operation of the unconscious. Elijah is the personification of the cognitional element, Salome of the erotic. Elijah is the figure of the old prophet filled with wisdom. One could speak of these two figures as personifications of Logos and Eros very specifically shaped. This is practical for intellectual play, but as Logos and Eros are purely speculative terms, not scientific in any sense, but irrational, it is very much better to leave the figures as they are, namely as events, experiences.

As to the snake, what is its further significance?[7]

[6] Cf. *MDR*, p. 182/174, and CW 5, index, s.vv. hero; snake(s)—mostly as originally in *Wandlungen und Symbole*.

[7] Cf. pp. 90 and 92.

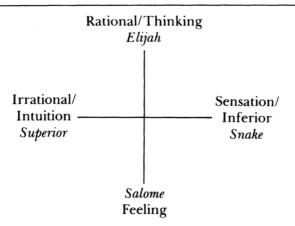

LECTURE 12

8 June 1925

Dr. Ward's question: "You speak of energy as falling from a higher to a lower level and use the waterfall as the illustration. How do you account for the opposing though equal energy that lifts the water to the rain cloud? In this case is the rain cloud the lower level? It is if you transform your level into terms of heat energy. Should we not take into consideration in psychic energy this transformability into various modes of expression? Is not this the crux of the problem of the neurosis? If the psychic energy were sufficiently free or fluid to make easy transformations, the neurosis would not occur. But here enters the problem of ethics—the choice of direction. Will you kindly discuss this question?"

Dr. Jung: To make water rise from the sea you need new energy. When water runs uphill there is always an additional source of energy; in other words, the energy of the sun lifts it. Water lifted to the clouds must fall again. In the collective unconscious we release additional sources of energy that make our level rise. In the collective unconscious there is energy in "solid" forms from of old, but it is additional energy similar to the energy found in coal mines, and like the energy in the mines, it is subject to exhaustion. If we do not succeed in releasing atomic energy,[1] or the energy of the tides or the wind, the population of Europe will have to decrease. If we release the energy of the collective unconscious until we have no more, then we arrive at differentiation. The archetypes are sources of energy. If people who have no views of life catch hold of an archetypal idea, say a religious idea, they become efficient. Put an idea into the heads of small people and they become big and tremendously efficient.

[1] *Sic* (1925). The process of nuclear fission was discovered in 1938.

We like to think that with moral ideas we can direct our lives, but these things do not catch; if they did we would have been all right long ago. Moral views do not touch the collective unconscious. Within the realm of willpower we have choice, but beyond that no choice at all.

LECTURE

The black serpent symbolizes the introverting libido. Salome is the anima and Elijah the wise old man. Salome, being instinctive and quite blind, needs the foreseeing eyes of wisdom that Elijah possesses. The figure of the prophet is compensatory to that of the blind anima.[2]

As I am an introverted intellectual my anima contains feeling [that is] quite blind. In my case the anima contains not only Salome, but some of the serpent, which is sensation as well. As you remember, the real Salome was involved in incestuous relations with Herod, her stepfather, and it was because of the latter's love for her that she was able to get the head of John the Baptist.[3]

I had read much mythology before this fantasy came to me, and all of this reading entered into the condensation of these figures. The old man is a very typical figure. One encounters him everywhere; he appears in all sorts of forms, and usually in company with a young girl. (See Rider Haggard: *Wisdom's Daughter*.)[4]

Feeling-sensation is in opposition to the conscious intellect plus intuition, but the balance is insufficient. When you assume the anima is due to the preponderance of the differentiated function in the conscious, the unconscious is balanced by a figure within itself that compensates the anima figure. This is the old man Elijah. It is as though you have a scale, and in the one side of the scale is the conscious, in the other the unconscious. This was one of my first hypotheses. With Freud, the unconscious is always pouring out unacceptable material

[2] Cf. *MDR*, p. 182/174.

[3] Cf. Matthew 14:6ff. and Mark 6:22ff. In neither place, however, is the woman named. The identification is in Flavius Josephus, *Antiquities of the Jews*, XVIII, ch. 5. Jung's library contained a 1735 edition (in German) of the works of Josephus, which was inscribed "Dr. Jung," presumably Jung's father or grandfather. Jung affixed his own Ex Libris, 1889, when he was fourteen. (Personal communication from Lorenz Jung.)

[4] London, 1923. Cf. "Mind and Earth" (1927; CW 10), par. 75.

into the conscious, and the conscious has difficulty in taking up this material and represses it, and there is no balance.

In those days I saw a compensatory principle that seemed to show a balance between the conscious and unconscious. But I saw later that the unconscious was balanced in itself. It is the yea and the nay. The unconscious is not at all exactly the opposite of the conscious. It may be irrationally different. You cannot deduce the unconscious from the conscious. The unconscious is balanced in itself, as is the conscious. When we meet an extravagant figure like Salome, we have a compensating figure in the unconscious. If there were only such an evil figure as Salome, the conscious would have to build up a fence to keep this back, an exaggerated, fanatical, moral attitude. But I had not this exaggerated moral attitude, so I suppose that Salome was compensated by Elijah. When Elijah told me he was always with Salome, I thought it was almost blasphemous for him to say this. I had the feeling of diving into an atmosphere that was cruel and full of blood.

This atmosphere was around Salome, and to hear Elijah declare that he was always in that company shocked me profoundly. Elijah and Salome are together because they are pairs of opposites. Elijah is an important figure in man's unconscious, not in woman's. He is the man with prestige, the man with a low threshold of consciousness or with remarkable intuition. In higher society he would be the wise man; compare Lao-tse. He has the ability to get into touch with archetypes. He will be surrounded with mana, and will arouse other men because he touches the archetypes in others. He is fascinating and has a thrill about him. He is the wise man, the medicine man, the mana man.

Later on in evolution, this wise man becomes a spiritual image, a god, "the old one from the mountains" (compare Moses coming down from the mountain as lawgiver), the sorcerer of the tribe. He is the legislator. Even Christ was in company with Moses and Elijah in his transfiguration. All great lawgivers and masters of the past, such as for example the Mahatmas of theosophical teaching, are thought of by theosophists as spiritual factors still in existence.[5] Thus the Dalai Lama is supposed by theosophists to be such a figure. In the his-

[5] The Mahatmas, or Masters, are believed to be spiritual teachers dwelling in Tibet who founded theosophy. Other great religious teachers are also identified as Masters. Cf. B. F. Campbell, *Ancient Wisdom Revived: A History of the Theosophical Movement* (Berkeley, 1980), pp. 53–54. For Jung's skepticism about theosophy, cf. *Types* (CW 6), par. 594, and *Dream Analysis*, pp. 56, 60.

tory of Gnosis, this figure plays a great role, and every sect claims to have been founded by such a one. Christ is not quite suitable; he is too young to be the Mahatma. The great man has to be given another role. John the Baptist was the great wise man, teacher, and initiator, but he has been depotentiated. The same archetype reappears in Goethe as Faust and as Zarathustra in Nietzsche, where Zarathustra came as a visitation. Nietzsche has been gripped by the sudden animation of the great wise man. This plays an important role in man's psychology, as I have said, but unfortunately a less important part than that played by the anima.

The serpent is the animal, but the magical animal. There is hardly anyone whose relation to a snake is neutral. When you think of a snake, you are always in touch with racial instinct. Horses and monkeys have snake phobia, as man has. In primitive countries, you can easily see why man has acquired this instinct. The Bedouins are afraid of scorpions and carry amulets to protect themselves, especially stones from certain Roman ruins. So whenever a snake appears, you must think of a primordial feeling of fear. The black color goes with this feeling, and also with the subterranean character of the snake. It is hidden and therefore dangerous. As animal it symbolizes something unconscious; it is the instinctive movement or tendency; it shows the way to the hidden treasure, or it guards the treasure. The dragon is the mythological form of the snake. The snake has a fascinating appeal, a peculiar attraction through fear. Some people are fascinated by this fear. Things that are awe-inspiring and dangerous have an extraordinary attraction. This combination of fear and attraction is shown, for instance, when a bird is hypnotized by a snake, for the bird flutters down to fight the snake, and then becomes attracted and held by the snake. The serpent shows the way to hidden things and expresses the introverting libido, which leads man to go beyond the point of safety, and beyond the limits of consciousness, as expressed by the deep crater.

The snake is also Yin, the dark female power. The Chinese would not use the snake (i.e., dragon) as a symbol for Yin, but for Yang. In Chinese [tradition], the Yin is symbolized by the tiger and the Yang by the dragon.

The serpent leads the psychological movement apparently astray into the kingdom of shadows, dead and wrong images, but also into the earth, into concretization. It makes things real, makes them come into being, after the manner of Yin. Inasmuch as the serpent leads into the shadows, it has the function of the anima; it leads you into the depths, it connects the above and the below. There are mythological parallels. Certain Negroes call the soul "My serpent"—they say, "My serpent said to me," meaning "I had an idea." Therefore the serpent is also the symbol of wisdom, speaks the wise word of the depths. It is quite chthonic, quite earth-born, like Erda, daughter of the earth. The dead heroes transform into serpents in the underworld.

In mythology, that which had been the sun-bird devours itself, goes into the earth, and comes up again. The Semenda Bird,[6] like the phoenix, burns in order to renew itself. Out of the ashes comes the snake, and out of the snake the bird again. The snake is the transition from the Heaven-born, back again to the bird. The snake encoils the vessel of Ra. In the Night Journey, in the Seventh Hour, Ra must fight the serpent. Ra is supported by the ritual of the priests: if he kills the serpent, the sun rises, if he should not succeed, the sun would rise no more.

The serpent is the personification of the tendency to go into the depths and to deliver oneself over to the alluring world of shadows.

I had already engaged the old man in an interesting conversation; and, quite against all expectations, the old man had assumed a rather critical attitude toward my kind of thinking. He said I treated thoughts as if I generated them myself, but, according to his views, thoughts were like animals in a forest, or people in a room, or birds in the air. He said, "If you should see people in a room, you would not say that you made those people, or that you were responsible for them." Only then I learned psychological objectivity. Only then could I say to a patient, "Be quiet, something is happening." There *are* such things as mice in a house. You cannot say you are wrong when you have a thought. For the understanding of the unconscious we must see our thoughts as events, as phenomena. We must have perfect objectivity.

A few evenings later, I felt that things should continue; so again I tried to follow the same procedure, but *it* would not descend. I remained on the surface. Then I realized I had a conflict in myself about going down, but I could not make out what it was, I only felt that two dark principles were fighting each other, two serpents. There was a mountain ridge, a knife edge, on one side a sunny desert country, on the other side darkness. I saw a white snake on the light side and a dark snake on the dark side. They met in battle on the

---

[6] Cf. "Concerning Mandala Symbolism" (1950; CW 9 i), par. 685.

narrow ridge. A dreadful conflict ensued. Finally the head of the black snake turned white, and it retired, defeated. I felt, "Now we can go on." Then the old man appeared high up on the rocky ridge. We went far up, and reached a cyclopean wall, boulders piled up in a great ring. I thought, "Ha, this is a Druidic sacred place." We entered through an opening, and found ourselves in a large place, with a mound[ed] Druid altar. The old man climbed up on the altar. At once he became small and so did the altar, while the walls grew bigger and bigger. Then I saw a tiny house near the walls, and a tiny, tiny woman, like a doll, who turned out to be Salome. I also saw the snake, but it too was very tiny. The walls kept on growing, and then I realized that I was in the underworld, that the walls were those of a crater, and that this was the house of Salome and Elijah. All this time, I did not grow, but kept my own size. As the walls grew, Salome and Elijah grew a bit bigger. I realized that I was at the bottom of the world. Elijah smiled and said, "Why, it is just the same, above or below."

Then a most disagreeable thing happened. Salome became very interested in me, and she assumed that I could cure her blindness. She began to worship me. I said, "Why do you worship me?" She replied, "You are Christ." In spite of my objections she maintained this. I said, "This is madness," and became filled with skeptical resistance. Then I saw the snake approach me. She came close and began to encircle me and press me in her coils. The coils reached up to my heart. I realized as I struggled, that I had assumed the attitude of the Crucifixion. In the agony and the struggle, I sweated so profusely that the water flowed down on all sides of me. Then Salome rose, and she could see. While the snake was pressing me, I felt that my face had taken on the face of an animal of prey, a lion or a tiger.

The interpretation of these dreams is this: First the fight of the two snakes: the white means a movement into the day, the black into the kingdom of darkness, with moral aspects too. There was a real conflict in me, a resistance to going down. My stronger tendency was to go up. Because I had been so impressed the day before with the cruelty of the place I had seen, I really had a tendency to find a way to the conscious by going up, as I did on the mountain. The mountain was the kingdom of the sun, and the ring-wall was the vessel in which people had gathered the sun.

Elijah had said that it was just the same below or above. Compare

Dante's *Inferno*.[7] The Gnostics express this same idea in the symbol of the reversed cones. Thus the mountain and the crater are similar. There was nothing of conscious structure in these fantasies, they were just events that happened. So I assume that Dante got his ideas from the same archetypes. I have seen these ideas very often in patients—the upper and the lower cones, things above and things below.

Salome's approach and her worshiping of me is obviously that side of the inferior function which is surrounded by an aura of evil. I felt her insinuations as a most evil spell. One is assailed by the fear that perhaps this is madness. This is how madness begins, this *is* madness. For example, in a certain Russian book there is a story of a man who fears he will go mad.[8] Lying in bed at night, he sees a bright square of moonlight in the middle of the room. He says to himself, "If I should sit there and howl like a dog, then I would be mad, but I am not doing it so I am not mad." Then he tries to dismiss this thought, but after a while he says to himself, "I might sit there and howl like a dog, knowing it and choosing it, and still I would not be mad." Again he tries to put the thought away, but finally he can resist it no longer—he gets up and sits in the moonlight and howls like a dog, and then he *is* mad.

You cannot get conscious of these unconscious facts without giving yourself to them. If you can overcome your fear of the unconscious and can let yourself down, then these facts take on a life of their own. You can be gripped by these ideas so that you really go mad, or nearly so. These images have so much reality that they recommend themselves, and such extraordinary meaning that one is caught. They form part of the ancient mysteries; in fact, it is such figures that made the mysteries. Compare the mysteries of Isis as told in Apuleius,[9] with the initiation and deification of the initiate.

Awe surrounds the mysteries, particularly the mystery of deification. This was one of the most important of the mysteries; it gave the immortal value to the individual—it gave certainty of immortality.

---

[7] The reference is to Dante's conception of the conical form of the cavity of Hell, with its circles, mirroring in reverse the form of Heaven, with its spheres.

[8] The story, as related, could not be located in any Russian writer, though Slavic scholars who were consulted agree that it may be a garbled recollection of a story, "The Whistle," by Leonid Andreyev.

[9] Lucius Apuleius, *The Golden Ass*, XI. Cf. *Symbols of Transformation* (CW 5), par. 102, n. 51; *Psychology of the Unconscious* (1916), p. 496, n. 30.

One gets a peculiar feeling from being put through such an initiation. The important part that led up to the deification was the snake's encoiling of me. Salome's performance was deification. The animal face which I felt mine transformed into was the famous [Deus] Leontocephalus of the Mithraic mysteries,[10] the figure which is represented with a snake coiled around the man, the snake's head resting on the man's head, and the face of the man that of a lion. This statue has only been found in the mystery grottoes (the underchurches, the last remnants of the catacombs). The catacombs were not originally places of concealment, but were chosen as symbolical of a descent into the underworld. It was also part of those early conceptions that the saints should be buried with the martyrs in order to go down into the earth before rising again. The Dionysian mysteries have the same idea.

When the catacombs decayed, the idea of the church continued. The Mithraic religion also had an underground church, and only initiates assisted at the underground ceremonies. Holes were cut in the walls of the underground portion in order that lay people might hear in the church above what was being said by the initiates in the church below. The lower church was fitted up with divans or cubicles placed opposite each other. Bells were used in the ceremony, and bread marked with a cross. We know that they celebrated a sacramental meal where this bread was eaten with water instead of wine. The Mithraic cult was strictly ascetic. No women were admitted as members. It is almost certain that the symbolical rite of deification played a part in these mysteries.

The lion-headed god encoiled by the snake was called Aion, or the eternal being. He derives from a Persian deity, Zrwanakarana,[11] which word means "the infinitely long duration." Another very interesting symbol in this cult is the Mithraic amphora with flame arising from it, and the lion on one side with the snake on the other, both trying to get at the fire.[12] The lion is the young, hot, dry July sun in culmination of light, the summer. The serpent is humidity, darkness, the earth, winter. They are the opposites of the world trying to come together with the reconciling symbol between them. It is the famous symbolism of the vessel, a symbolism that survives till 1925—see *Parsifal*. It is the Holy Grail, called the Vase of Sin (see King: *The Gnostics*

[10] Cf. CW 5, par. 425, and pl. XLIV; *Psychology of the Unconscious*, pp. 313f.
[11] Ibid.
[12] Cf. CW 5, pl. LXIII.

and Their Remains[13]). Also it is a symbol of the early Gnostics. It is of course a man's symbol, a symbol of the womb—the creative womb of the man out of which rises the fire. When the pairs of opposites come together, something divine happens, and then it is immortality, the eternal, creative time. Wherever there is generation there is time, therefore Chronos is God of Time, Fire, and Light.

In this deification mystery you make yourself into the vessel, and are a vessel of creation in which the opposites reconcile. The more these images are realized, the more you will be gripped by them. When the images come to you and are not understood, you are in the society of the gods or, if you will, the lunatic society; you are no longer in human society, for you cannot express yourself. Only when you can say, "This image is so and so," only then do you remain in human society. Anybody could be caught by these things and lost in them—some throw the experience away saying it is all nonsense, and thereby losing their best value, for these are the creative images. Another may identify himself with the images and become a crank or a fool.

Question: What is the date of this dream?

Dr. Jung: December 1913. All this is Mithraic symbolism from beginning to end. In 1910 I had a dream[14] of a Gothic cathedral in which Mass was being celebrated. Suddenly the whole side wall of the cathedral caved in, and herds of cattle, with ringing bells, trooped into the church. You may remember that Cumont[15] remarks that if something had happened to disrupt Christianity in the third century, the world would be Mithraic today.

[13] C. W. King, *The Gnostics and Their Remains, Ancient and Medieval* (London, 1864)—in Jung's library.

[14] Not recorded (other than in Joan Corrie, *A B C of Jung's Psychology*, 1927, p. 80, where it is reported as from this seminar). In a letter to Freud, 20 Feb. 1910, Jung wrote: "All sorts of things are cooking in me, mythology in particular. . . . My dreams revel in symbols that speak volumes."

[15] Franz Cumont, *Textes et monuments figurés relatifs aux mystères de Mithra* (2 vols., Brussels, 1894–1899), and *Die Mysterien des Mithra* (1911)—both in Jung's library, as are other works by Cumont. Jung's interest in Mithraism is mentioned as early as June 1910 in his correspondence with Freud: cf. letters 199a F and 200 J. He cited Cumont frequently in *Wandlungen und Symbole*.

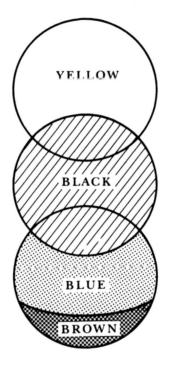

Diagram 1

LECTURE 13

15 June 1925

Dr. Jung:

I have brought with me some pictures done by a young American who, at the time that he made the pictures, had no knowledge of my theories. I merely told him to try to express in color the inner condition of his mind, which was very badly muddled. He had no prescription as to the style in which he should paint, and I explained very little about the pictures to him so as not to disturb the naïveté of his attitude about them.

The pictures follow a progressive series and, as you will see, are a further expression of the transcendent function, that is, an effort to make the unconscious content conscious. They show a struggle between the pairs of opposites, with an attempt to solve the problem of bringing the two together, and so they really belong to the discussion we had of the pairs of opposites, but I was not able to get them before today.

First picture (see Diagram 1):[1] In this picture he said he felt clearness above; below, something moving or snakelike, and then the weight of the earth; in between was emptiness, blackness. We might observe in passing that only an American could produce a symbol like this. The blue in the top part of the lowest circle is associated with the sea—he actually does feel he is at sea in his present condition. The black, the unconscious, is associated with the idea of evil. This picture is typical of masculine psychology: consciousness above, sex below, nothing in the middle.

Second picture: Two circles separate, one above and one below.

[1] Only the first picture is reproduced in the original transcript. The originals have not survived.

This shows a complete division, Yang above and Yin below. In the lower circle a tendency to develop primitive ornamentation is shown.

Third picture: Shows an attempt to get things together. Yang colors above, Yin below, some signs of growth shown in an effort to depict a tree green in color. Snakes are coming up from below.

Fourth picture: Here is a very vigorous attempt at getting things together. The two principles, Yang and Yin, join in a starlike figure. The problem of intuition-sensation is shown in a vertical form of design. As soon as horizontal forms show in design it is the appearance of the rational functions, because they are on our earth.

Fifth picture: Here is shown a more typical Indian or primitive character. "Soul-birds" are shown; helpful animals are needed. In previous designs he came to an impossibility because a rational function cannot be taken up directly by an irrational type; therefore he has birds. The Yang has almost disappeared, the birds are in the center. In the earth peculiar movement is shown: canals, snakes, roots perhaps. Birds show an instinctive tendency. If he can see that there are some helpful birds about, that means more to him than any rational function.

Sixth picture: In the previous picture he approached the earth sphere. Here he is deeply in it. The earth reaches up to heaven, the clouds hide the sun, but Yang descends into the earth, deep into the sea. High up there is a man who is looking to see if he can jump down into the depths of the unconscious. The unconscious contents are felt as fishes. There is no connection between the man's standpoint and the depths; he cannot take the leap.

Seventh picture: Here the man has taken the leap. But it is air, not water; it is a desert, skulls are present. The man is fastened to the bottom with iron balls. All life is shown above. This means that the going to the other extreme is as disastrous and full of death as if he had remained above. He is in the bowels of the earth.

The production of these pictures is a stimulation of the primitive layers of the mind, and the individual will get at instinctive impulses thereby. The pictures show a marked influence from the East, which is generally characteristic of American psychology as opposed to European. No European could have produced these drawings.

(There followed some discussion as to the ways in which the various races tend to react toward the primitive cultures with which they come in contact.)

North and South America have followed very different ways in this respect. The Anglo-Saxon holds himself away from the primitive, while the Latin goes down to his level. I have come into contact with some very strange psychological problems illustrating this. The following will show you something of what happens in South America.

I was once consulted by a South American family as to the condition of their son, who had been nearly driven crazy by his friends. The parents were Austrian and went to South America only after their marriage. Inside their house European traditions prevailed, but outside everything was Indian, the Latin inhabitants not having resisted those influences. It was the custom for the Indian families to send their children into the city to work for little or no wages, and in the case of the little girl this meant inevitable sexual abuse.

This way of life got terribly on the nerves of the son of these Austrians, and he went to a professor of whom he was very fond to ask him for advice. The professor asked him if he had a mascot, and of course the boy had none, so he was given one. The professor told him he had to take this mascot, which was a doll, and attend to the task of increasing its strength all the time, and the stronger the doll got, the more the boy's troubles would diminish. The first thing he had to do with it was to carry it about the streets in his arms, and this the boy did, though with great shame. Then he took it to the professor and asked him if there was anything more to be done, and was told there was. The doll was not yet strong enough. He must take it to a great celebration that was about to be held for the president of the republic and he must break through the cordon of police and swing the doll three times in the face of the president. The boy did this and of course got into trouble with the police, but was set free when they found that the affair had only to do with the strengthening of a mascot. The boy went back to the professor. No, the doll was not yet as strong as it ought to be! He must now find a little girl and throttle her over the doll until she was nearly dead. Then the force of her agony as she approached death would go into the doll and it would be really strong. The boy broke down after this last ordeal, but he was afraid to say anything, for if he did all the strength would go out of the doll, and so he continued in a thoroughly neurotic condition till his parents had to seek help.

The boy's mother was Catholic, but it would be absurd to say that the Church supported such things. The Spanish clergy is and always has been terribly superstitious in these Latin American countries. One can find things such as I have described going on in all of them, and it comes from the fact that the Conquistadores mixed with the natives in marriage. In doing this the Latins have managed to keep out of the split between the conscious and the unconscious, but have lost their superiority. The Anglo-Saxons did not mix with the primitives, but in the unconscious they sank down to the primitive level.

Miss Taylor's question: (1) "Do you think that some development of the Mithraic religion may become a living religion in the near future?"

Dr. Jung: I could not assume that anything like that is going to happen. I merely mentioned the Mithraic religion because my fantasies were so much connected with it. In itself this religion is as antiquated as can be. It is only relatively important as being the brother of Christianity, which has assimilated some elements from it. It is interesting to trace out both those elements that were discarded and those that were accepted by Christianity. The ringing of the bells in the celebration of the Mass probably comes from the Mithraic cult, where bells were rung at a certain point in the mysteries. Also, Christmas day is a Mithraic feast. In early days, Christmas came on the 8th of January, and was a day taken over from the Egyptians, being the day celebrating the finding of the body of Osiris. It was only in later days, when the Mithraic cult was being overcome, that the Christians took the 25th of December, the day celebrated by the followers of Mithras as the day of *Sol invictus*, for their Christmas. To the early Christians, Christmas was the resurrection of the sun, and as late as Augustine, Christ was identified with the sun.

Miss Taylor's question: (2) "Is the view you expressed in your last lecture a further development of an earlier view that the contents of the unconscious can be deduced from what is lacking in the unconscious?"

Dr. Jung: Yes, but I do not mean to imply a contradiction between my earlier view and what I said the other day about the unconscious being balanced. I have simply gone one step further.

There is no doubt that to a certain extent the conscious can be deduced from the unconscious and vice versa. If a dream says such and such a thing, we are justified in saying the conscious attitude must have been thus and so. If a person is only intellectual he must have repressed feelings in the unconscious, and we have a right to expect to find them there.

I went on further to say that the unconscious shows a balance within itself, over and above the compensatory role it plays to the conscious. That is, we cannot say that the main contents of the unconscious are nothing but a balance to the conscious, nor vice versa. Therefore one can perfectly well live wholly in the conscious as most people do, and pay little or no attention to the unconscious. As long as you can put up with the symptoms and inhibitions that come from such a life, it does not matter.

Now the balance in the conscious consists in weighing processes. You say yea to this thing and nay to that. Similarly, if you take a dream, you can find a yea and a nay in that also—that is what I call the ambiguity of a dream; it is never wholeheartedly committed to one thing or the other, and so I speak of the unconscious as being balanced in itself when it is operating properly. In all cases where the unconscious is heavily one-sided, it is so because it is out of gear. A case in point is that of Saul and Paul—had Saul been more balanced in his conscious, his unconscious would have run a different course also, and would not have produced the full-fledged Paul overnight, so to speak.

One can follow this same principle of balance in any separate units holding a compensatory relation to one another—for example, in the relation of men and women to each other. There is no man who could not exist without a woman—that is, he carries the necessary balance within himself if he be obliged to live his life that way, and the same thing applies to a woman with respect to a man, but if either sex is to have a complete life, it requires the other as a compensatory side. It is the same thing with the conscious and the unconscious, and we seek analysis just to get at the benefits of the compensation from the unconscious. Primitives show a much more balanced psychology than we do for the reason that they have no objection to letting the irrational come through, while we resent it. Sometimes a patient becomes greatly outraged at the mere possibility of a dream or a fantasy having a sexual content, though to be sure, today it has become fashionable to recognize sexuality. But let a dream show a moral criticism about the individual—let it say there is something unclean and ugly about you—and there is the same violent reaction that used to come with a sexual dream.

Mr. Robertson: Isn't there another way of looking at the balancing that goes on in the conscious? That is, if all four functions are in operation, does not that mean balance?

Dr. Jung: But even if all four functions are in operation, there are things that are forgotten, and the unconscious contains these. There is a tendency among some people to make the unconscious carry what properly belongs to the conscious, and this always upsets the functioning of the unconscious. Such people could remove much both from the personal and from the collective unconscious, and so free the unconscious to function more normally. For example, you can run across people who think themselves born without a religious sense, and this is just as absurd as if they said they were born without eyes. It simply means they have left all that side of themselves in the unconscious. If you get these things out of the unconscious into the conscious, then, as I said, the unconscious functions are helped. As another example, one is always hearing persons who have had some experience of analysis saying, "I won't make up my mind about that, I'll see what my dreams say." But there are hosts of things which call for decisions from the conscious, and about which it is idiotic to "put it up" to the unconscious for a decision.

This freeing of the unconscious of elements that really belong to the conscious is greatly aided by all the old mystery practices. All who go through the initiation ceremonies in the right spirit find a magic quality in them, which is simply due to the effect they have had upon the unconscious. One can develop astonishing insights through the release that comes to the unconscious in this way. One can even come to clairvoyance; but when such a gift as the latter is developed, it makes the person permeable to all sorts of atmospheric conditions that may result in his misery. When life becomes unbearably impoverished, people reach out for such extensions of powers, only to curse fate often when they have achieved them; but when one has fire, one welcomes the insight. Those of you who heard Dr. Radin's[2] last lecture remember the zigzag road that was encountered after the fourth lodge in the Medicine Dance had been passed. At the end of the fourth lodge the initiate has been given high honors and has won great increase of powers, and now the road becomes full of appalling obstacles. So when you relieve the unconscious of non-realized contents, you release it for its own special functioning, and it will go ahead like an animal. You will have the zigzag road with all the fears of the primitive to be met on it, but also you will have all the wealth of his experience. For it is a fact that, to the primitive, life is far more voluminous than to us, because there is not only the thing but also its meaning. We look at an animal and say it is such and such a species, but if we knew that animal to be our ghost brother, it would be a different situation for us. Or, we sit in the woods and a beetle drops

[2] Records of Radin's talks have not been discovered, but it is evident here that a subject was the Medicine Rite of the Winnebago tribe, of the American Middle West. Cf. Radin, *The Road of Life and Death: A Ritual Drama of the American Indians* (B.S. V; New York, 1945). For an account of Radin's relations with Jung and how he happened to attend the seminar, see the Introduction, above.

down on someone's head. "What a nuisance," is all the comment it elicits, but to the primitive there is meaning in that event. Sometimes I have met this primitive reaction in my patients—an extraordinary sense of the meaningfulness of apparently trivial things in nature. After all, an animal is not just a thing with fur on it; it is a complete being. You may say a coyote is nothing but a coyote, but then along comes one that is Dr. Coyote, a super-animal who has mana and spiritual powers. So says the primitive.

The unconscious should act for us like a super-animal. When one dreams of a bull, one should not think of it as being below the human only, but also as being above—that is, as of something godlike.

*

Miss Houghton: If it is permissible to ask the question here, I would like to know why Americans are closer to the Far East than Europeans.

Dr. Jung: First, they are closer geographically, and secondly there are much stronger art connections of the East with America than with Europe, and then Americans are living on the soil of that race.

Miss Houghton: Do you mean ethnologically?

Dr. Jung: Yes. I was enormously struck by the resemblance of the Indian women of the Pueblos to the Swiss women in Canton Appenzell, where we have descendants of Mongolian invaders. These might be ways of explaining the fact that something in American psychology leans toward the East.

Dr. de Angulo: Is not that to be explained from the conscious?

Dr. Jung: Yes, it might be explained that way too. That is, Americans, being so split, turn to the East for the expression of the unconscious. The appreciation of the Chinese in America is extraordinary. All my knowledge of Chinese things comes from the Anglo-Saxon side, not from Europe—from England, it is true, but America is an extension of England.

LECTURE

I want to give you today a scheme for understanding such figures as I spoke of last time, that is, the anima and the wise old man. When you analyze a man, you almost always come to these figures if you go deep enough. At first you might not have them separated—I had three figures—but you might get them fused with an animal, say with a feminine form. Or the animal can be split off, and there can be a hermaphroditic figure. Then the old man and the anima are one.

All these figures correspond to certain relations of the conscious ego to the persona, and the symbolism varies according to conscious conditions. Let us start with this diagram [2].

Take this room as consciousness: I feel myself as a luminous point in this conscious field of vision. I am not aware of what you think, so it is a field limited in extent—outside it is the world of tangible reality. This world can be represented to me through an object; thus, if I ask Mr. A. something he becomes my bridge to that world for that specific instant. But if I ask myself how I establish an absolute or unconditioned connection with the world, my answer is that I can only do that when I am both passive and active at the same time, as much victim as actor. This only occurs for a man through woman. She is the factor that links man to the earth. If you do not marry you may go where you please, but as soon as a man marries, he must be in some particular spot, he must put down roots.

This field of vision of which I speak is my sphere of action, and as far as my action extends, I extend my sphere of influence. This makes my mask, but when I am active, my action can only get to you by your receiving it, thus you help make my appearance—I cannot make it alone. In other words, I create a shell around me due to my

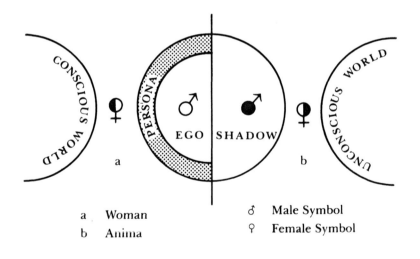

a   Woman   ♂   Male Symbol
b   Anima   ♀   Female Symbol

Diagram 2

influence on you and yours on me. This we call persona. The fact that there is a shell is no intentional deception; it is simply due to the fact that a system of relationships is there whereby I am never apart from the effect of the object on me. Insofar as you live in a world, you cannot escape forming a persona. You can say, "I won't have such and such a persona," but as you discard one you get another— unless, of course, you live on Everest. You can only learn who you are through your effects on other people. By this means you create your personality. So much for the conscious.

On the unconscious side, we have to work by inference through dreams. We must assume a field of vision somewhat the same, but a little peculiar since one is never exactly oneself in dreams; even sex is not always clearly defined in the unconscious. We can assume that there are things in the unconscious also, namely images of the collective unconscious. What is your relationship to these things? Again it is a woman. If you give up the woman in reality, you fall a victim to the anima. It is this feeling of inevitability about his connection with woman that man dislikes the most. Just when he is sure he has cut himself free of her and is moving about at last in an inner world which is his own, behold, he is in his mother's lap!

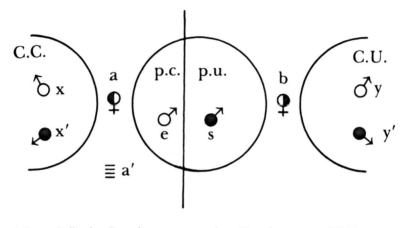

C.C. = Collective Conscious.	y′ = Negative aspect of C.U.
p.c. = Personal conscious.	a = Real woman or absolute object.
p.u. = Personal unconscious.	a′ = Plurality of absolute objects.
C.U. = Collective Unconscious.	b = Anima.
x = Positive aspect of C.C.	e = Ego.
x′ = Negative aspect of C.C.	s = Shadow self.
y = Positive aspect of C.U.	

Diagram 3

Dr. Jung:

I will continue the discussion begun last time, using a similar diagram (see Diagram 3). As I have tried to show by the dark and light coloring in *a* and *b*, a man has both positive and negative relations to the real woman and to the anima. Usually if his attitude toward the real woman be positive, then his attitude toward the anima is negative, and vice versa. But it very often happens that he has a positive and a negative attitude toward the woman at the same time, only the negative is buried and must be sought out from the depths of the unconscious. It is often to be observed in marriages, for example, that this negative factor starts out as something quite negligible, and then with the years becomes the most patent thing about the relationship, until finally the break comes, though all the while the two people have had the illusion of a most harmonious marriage.

We find the principle of duality in man's collective conscious, as I have tried to show in the double symbols *x* and *x'*. That is, in general our laws and ideals are good, so when we begin to investigate man's conscious world, we come first on the positive symbol *x*. If we go through history we can be greatly impressed with the scope and magnitude of the things developed in church and state. If we were to speak in terms of primitive men, we would say there was a wise council of elders that had seen to these things. Let us take as a sample the Catholic Mass. If we study this we must recognize it to be one of the most perfect things we possess. Similarly with our laws, there are many aspects of them that must excite our respect and admiration. But that does not complete the picture; we cannot escape the fact that these things have also a very evil side. Take the goodness expressed in Christianity, for instance. That is apparent to us, but get outside of your own skin and into that of a Polynesian native, and Christianity looks very black indeed. Or ask the Spanish heretics who have been burned for the glory of God what they think of Christianity.

Turning to the side of the unconscious, the duality of the anima figure is obvious. When a man knows his anima, she is both night and day to him. As we have so often observed in connection with Rider Haggard's "She," the classic anima figure, we can never be too sure either of her goodness or of her evilness; now it is the one, now the other that grips us. Her potency lies in large measure in the duality of her nature. A man may, as I have said, know the real woman also as lightness and darkness, but when he sees in a woman the magical quality that is the essence of She, he at once begins tremendous projections of the unconscious upon her.

There is duality also in a man's relation to the collective unconscious. Passing through the anima into the collective unconscious one comes to the figure of the wise old man, the shaman or medicine man. In general, the medicine man has a very beneficent side. If cattle are lost, he must know how and where to find them; if there is need of rain, he must see that it is made. Then he must also undertake the cure of disease. In all these purposes he appears as a positive figure, as I have shown in the diagram by y. But there is black magic to be taken into account, and this is closely associated with evil, so that one often has y', which we can call the black magician, split off from y.

This dual aspect in which a man's collective unconscious can present itself was brought very vividly to my attention through the dream of a young divinity student about whom I was once consulted.[1] He was in a conflict of doubts as to whether he had chosen right in becoming a minister, as to whether he really believed as he thought he did, etc. Many of you, however, have heard this dream before, so I do not know that it is worthwhile for me to repeat it.

(It was requested that the dream be repeated.)

Well then, the dreamer found himself in the presence of a very beautiful venerable old man who was clad in a black robe. He knew

---

[1] Jung first mentioned this dream in the third of three lectures he delivered in London, 1924, under the auspices of the New Education Fellowship: the first, on 10 May, as part of a conference of local educational societies at the British Empire Exhibition, recently opened in the suburb of Wembley; the second and third, on 12 and 13 May, at the Mortimer Street Hall, in the West End. (*Times Educational Supplement*, 3, 10, and 17 May, 1924.) The lectures had originally been drafted by Jung in English and revised by C. Roberts Aldrich; they were published first in German (1926), then in English in *Contributions to Analytical Psychology* (1928), translated (other than these lectures) by H. G. Baynes and Cary F. (de Angulo) Baynes. For the dream discussed here, see "Analytical Psychology and Education" (CW 17), par. 208, and, in more detail, "Archetypes of the Collective Unconscious" (1934; CW 9 i), pars. 71ff.

this man was the White Magician. The old man had just finished a sort of discourse, which the dreamer knew was full of fine things, but he could not quite remember what had been said, though he did know the old man had said the Black Magician would be needed. Just then in came another very beautiful old man dressed in white, and this was the Black Magician. He wanted to speak to the White Magician but, seeing the young man there, hesitated. Then the White Magician immediately explained that the young man was "an innocent," and that the Black Magician could speak quite freely before him. So the Black Magician related that he came from a country where there was an old king reigning, and this old king, bethinking himself of approaching death, began to look about for a suitable and dignified grave in which he should be buried. Among some old monuments he came upon a very beautiful tomb, which he caused to be opened and cleaned. Within they found the grave of a virgin who had lived ages and ages ago. When they threw out the bones and these came into the sunlight, they immediately formed themselves into a black horse which ran away into the desert and was lost. The Black Magician said he had heard about this horse and thought it very important to find him, so he went back to the place where all this had taken place, and there he found the horse's tracks. These he followed into the desert, and for days and days, until he came to the other side of the desert, and there he found the black horse grazing. By his side lay the keys to Paradise. With these he had come to the White Magician for help, as he did not know what to do with them.

This was the dream of a man quite untouched by analytical ideas. By himself he had come into problems that activated his unconscious in this way, and because he had an unrecognized poetic faculty, the unconscious content took this form, which without that faculty would not have been possible. Obviously the dream is full of wisdom, and had I analyzed the young man he would surely have been impressed with that wisdom, and come to have deep respect for the unconscious.

*

I would like now to try to present to you something about the psychology of women, using this same diagram, with a few changes (see Diagram 4).

We may say that the real man is seen by the woman on his bright side, and that her relationship to the real man is a comparatively exclusive one—that in this respect, it is just the opposite of the average

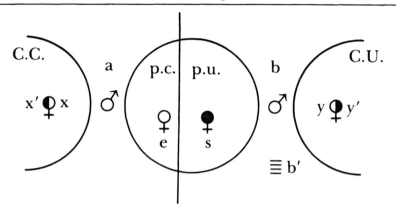

The symbols C.C., p.c., p.u., and C.U. remain the same as in Diagram 3.

x'x = Fused dual aspect of the Collective Conscious.
yy' = Fused dual aspect of the Collective Unconscious.
a = Real man or absolute object.
b = Animus.
b' = Plurality of animuses.

Diagram 4

relation of a man to the real woman. In a man this relationship is not exclusive. When the average man permits comparison of his wife with other women he says, "She is my wife among women." To the woman, though, the object that personifies the world to her (*a* in our diagram) is *my* husband, *my* children, in the midst of a relatively uninteresting world. This "unique" husband has a shadow side for the wife, just as we saw in the case of the man in relation to the real woman.

Similarly the animus has a bright and a dark side, but balancing the unique man in the conscious, we have in the unconscious of woman a multitude of animus figures. Man understands his relation to his anima as being a highly emotional affair, while woman's relation to her animus is more in the Logos field. When a man is possessed by his anima, he is under peculiar feelings, he cannot control his emotions, but is controlled by them. A woman dominated by her animus is one who is possessed by opinions. Nor is she too discriminating about these opinions. She can easily say, "In nineteen hundred and so and so, Papa said this to me," or, "Some years ago a man with a white beard told me this was true," and so it remains true for her into eternity. It is felt as a silent prejudice by a man who meets this phenomenon in a woman. It is something exceedingly baffling to him, and irritating to a degree through its power and invisibility.

Now then we come to the woman's relation to the collective conscious. Since I have not a woman's feelings, I am perhaps not competent to throw much light on what that relationship is, but inasmuch as the family seems the real basis of a woman's life, perhaps it would be fair to say that her attitude toward the world of the conscious is that of a mother. A woman too has a peculiar attitude toward nature, much more trusting than that of a man. She is always saying, "Oh, well that will come out all right," just when a man is ready to explode with anxiety. There must be something like this to account for the fact that there are three times more suicides among men than among women. But we can always find that, though there is not the marked split in the woman's relation to the collective conscious that occurs in man, still there is enough of duality to permit us to make a symbol such as $x'x$. In other words, the woman sees that the dear old god who is going to make everything come out all right has moods of his own, so one must not be too trusting. This is the element of skepticism, the shadow side. Men tend to separate x and x'. Women tend to take them together. If you listen to an argument between men you can always hear them keeping the negative and the positive aspects of the subject distinct; they may discuss now the one, now the other. But begin an argument with a woman in which the premise carries in it this principle of discrimination, and in about two minutes she has shot through your whole logical structure by bringing the positive right into the middle field of the negative aspect and vice versa. Nor can you ever persuade her that she has thus destroyed the logic of the discussion. To her way of thinking, the two belong very close together. This struggle for a principle of unity runs through all her psychological processes, just as the opposite principle, that of discrimination, runs through those of man.

Now when it comes to the unconscious of the woman, the picture becomes obscure indeed. I think there again is to be found the figure of a mother, and again she has a dual aspect, but in a peculiar way. As we saw with man, he has the definite division into good and bad, Cosmos and Chaos, but in woman's collective unconscious it is a fusion of the human with the animal. I have been tremendously impressed with the animal character of the unconscious of woman, and I have reason to think that her relation to the Dionysian element is a very strong one. It looks to me as if man were really further away from the animal than the woman—not that he has not a strong animal likeness in him, but it is not so psychological as in women. It is as though in men the animal likeness stopped at the spinal cord while in women it extends into the lower strata of the brain, or that man keeps the animal kingdom in him below the diaphragm, while in women it extends throughout her being. When man sees this fact in women, he immediately assumes that the animal nature of women is exactly like his own, the only difference being that she has more of it. But that is altogether a mistake, for their animalness contains spirituality, while in the man it is only brute. The animal side of woman is probably like that we would find in any such an animal as the horse, if we could see such an animal from within itself instead of just from the outside as we do see it. If we were viewing the psychic life of a horse from within, it would appear very strange to us. But a man is always looking at an animal from the outside—he has not the psychic animalness in his unconscious that a woman has in hers.

Obviously, I have only been able to give you here an outline of the field of women's psychology. There are many questions that can arise in connection with it.

*

(There followed here a discussion that took two general lines: first the fact that men tended to separate the pairs of opposites, and women to preserve a relative union of them, and secondly, as to whether or not Dr. Jung had done justice to the degree of consciousness that women had achieved in their special world of feeling.

In connection with the first point it was said by Mr. Schmitz that it seemed to him the essential difference between men and women was that the woman had a sense of polarity given her by nature, while man got it through intellect—in other words that the woman was still unconscious and the man conscious, and that this was the basic idea of the presence of Helena, or the figure of an anima, with the old man.)

Dr. Jung: Yes, that is the way it appears to men, but you must always remember that a woman may have a kind of consciousness that a man does not understand, and out of this fact we have the typical mistakes a man makes about women. Helena is only a man's woman, she is what a man would wish, but not in the least what a woman would call a true woman—she is an artifact. A real woman is an altogether different person, and when a man runs against the latter and projects

Helena upon her, the thing simply doesn't fit, and disaster is inevitable.

*

Mr. Schmitz thought that there was nothing so strange in the kind of consciousness of women, only they had this inevitable tendency to mix things that should be kept separate.

Dr. Jung: But that again is a masculine prejudice. The kind of consciousness that man has developed tends toward splitting, or discrimination, but the principle of union which the woman holds to is not necessarily merely a state of unconsciousness, as you would imply, though it is perfectly true that in general women often do show a reluctance to becoming conscious.

*

(About the second point, namely as to whether Dr. Jung had done justice to the consciousness women had achieved in the world of feeling, it was said that, while he had shown very clearly the discriminations men had achieved in the field of the collective conscious, when it came to the woman in that field, he had rather left us with the impression that she was a hopelessly amorphous creature. It seemed to some of the class that, in order to have the picture complete, some more stress should have been laid on the fact that woman had built a world of feeling values in which she discriminated with as much nicety as man in the world of the intellect, and that it was just as confusing to her to have these feeling values trampled underfoot by the unfeeling man as often happened, as it was upsetting to the man to have his intellectual values "messed together" by the unthinking woman.)

LECTURE 15

29 June 1925

Dr. Jung:

Before taking up the questions, I would like to assign to the class a piece of work I am anxious to have it undertake: that is the analysis of three books written on the anima theme: *She*, by Haggard; *L'Atlantide*, by Benoît; and Meyrink's *Das grüne Gesicht.*[1] I would like you to choose three committees of about five people each for these three books, each committee selecting a chairman who will bring in the findings of the group. If you do this you will furnish me with a very good idea of what you have gained from these lectures. Of course you may proceed about it in any way you see fit, but I would like to make the following suggestions: (1) For the sake of the people in the class who may not have read the particular book under discussion, we should have a résumé of the contents; (2) then there should be a characterization and interpretation of the *dramatis personae*; (3) this should be followed by a presentation of the psychological processes involved, transformations of the libido, and behavior of the unconscious figures from start to finish. No doubt the presentation of the material will take about one hour, and then we should have about half an hour for discussion.

(It was suggested by the class that, instead of having all three books on anima problems, it would be interesting to have one that dealt with the animus. On Dr. Jung's recommendation, a novel called *The Evil Vineyard*, by Marie Hay,[2] was substituted for *Das grüne Gesicht*.)

[1] H. Rider Haggard, *She* (London, 1887); Pierre Benoît, *L'Atlantide* (Paris, 1920); Gustav Meyrink, *Das grüne Gesicht* (Leipzig, 1916). In his subsequent writings, Jung frequently cited the first two works as prime examples of the anima. He apparently had first encountered the novel *L'Atlantide* at the time of his trip to Algeria and Tunis in March 1920; cf. *Word and Image*, p. 151.

[2] New York and London, 1923. The Hon. Agnes Blanche Marie Hay (1873–19??),

The committees were chosen as follows (the chairman is indicated with §):

Dr. Harding§		Mr. Aldrich§		Dr. Mann§
Miss Baynes		Mrs. Zinno		Mr. Robertson
She Dr. Bond	*L'Atlan-*	Miss Houghton	*The Evil*	Miss Hincks
Mr. Radin	*tide*	Miss Sergeant	*Vineyard*	Mr. Bacon
Dr. Ward		Mr. Bacon		Dr. de Angulo

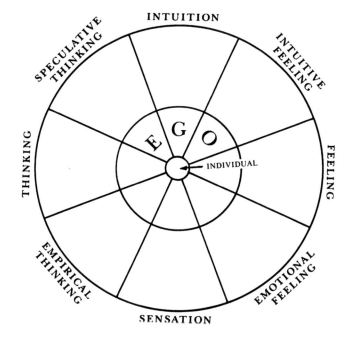

Diagram 5

an Englishwoman, married a German diplomat, Herbert Beneckendorff und von Hindenburg. Among her books was a critical life of the Swiss poet Gottfried Keller (1920). / For comment on the Hay, Haggard, and Benoît novels, cf. "Mind and Earth" (1927; CW 10), pars. 75–91. For the reports and discussion in the seminar, see below, following the appendix to Lecture 16.

Diagram 5 is of an ideal condition which we never meet in reality, that is, it presupposes a complete consciousness of all the functions. Therefore I have represented the functions on one plane. In the center is a virtual nucleus I call the self,⁴ which represents the totality or sum of the conscious and unconscious processes. This is in contradistinction to the ego or partial self, which is not conceived of as being in contact with the unconscious elements of the psychological processes. Because the ego is not in touch with the unconscious side of our personality—that is, not necessarily in touch with it—we very often have a very different idea of ourselves from what others have of us, even allowing for projections. The unconscious is continually playing its part, sometimes even an emphatic one, without our being cognizant of its imprint upon ourselves. I can do what in fact are really very complicated things without knowing that I have done them—as, for instance, in walking down the street, I may carefully weave my way in and out of a crowd of people, and yet if someone asks me at the end of a block or two, "How many people did you pass?" I am perfectly unable to say. Each of the people I have passed, however, has been registered separately in my mind; I simply have not brought the results to bear upon my ego.

Similarly, we seldom see to it that we become conscious of the expressions on our faces, and all the time things are peeping out from the unconscious that are perfectly visible to the outside observer, who sometimes finds it hard to realize our ignorance of the things that he can see so clearly. As long, then, as there remains so much in us that is not taken into account by the ego, the latter cannot be said to represent the totality of the mental processes.

Of course we cannot be too sure that we have this virtual center that I have assumed as existing; it is something that is not susceptible of proof. Instead of one center, we may have two or, as in dementia praecox, a multitude. But when you deal with a fairly normal individual there is always a center to which things lead up, and when something critical happens, it seems to come from that central government. Some people project the reaction they get from this central core of themselves as a God-given message. This center of self-regulation, then, is a postulate that is assumed.

---

³ Jung's classic presentation of his theory of the function types is found in *Types*, chapter X.

⁴ In the diagram, "individual."

I have represented the self as a point in the middle of the diagram, but it could just as well be thought of as including the whole, or indeed as spreading over all the world. Indian philosophy describes the self as I have taken it as being smaller than small, yet greater than great.

Turning to the diagram you will see that I have arranged the functions as sectors of the circle. Let us start with *thinking*,[5] or pure intellect. This as a rational function is connected with the irrational function *intuition* by what we call *speculative thinking*, or intuitive thinking. Then we pass to the polar opposite of thinking, namely *feeling*, through *intuitive feeling*, and from there to the polar opposite of intuition, *sensation*, via *emotion of feeling*. Emotion is that sort of feeling which is a physiological condition, and which is perceived by sensation. From sensation we get back again to *thinking* through a kind of thinking we call *empirical*, i.e., thinking to the fact. We have now the conception that thinking passes by easy transition to both intuition or sensation, or vice versa, but that it is furthest removed from feeling.

Let us now try to arrive at a precise notion of feeling, though, as we have observed in previous lectures, this is a task beset with difficulties. Will the class volunteer some suggestions as to the essential nature of feeling?

*

(The class volunteered one or two suggestions but, it must be said, with more enthusiasm for the theme than success in finding a solution. From one point of view there was an effort to define feeling in such a way that it should be shown to be present in all the other functions, from another point of view it was thought that the definition should be of such a character as to apply to feeling alone. It was generally agreed that the definition of feeling now accepted in analytical psychology—that is, as the function wherein subjective values are formulated—was not satisfactory, and that a satisfactory definition must include the ideal of a dynamic existing between subject and object. The end of the hour found the class still deep in this discussion. Dr. Jung was asked to give a brief summary of his viewpoint.)

Dr. Jung: My idea is that feeling is an unthinking kind of appreciation on the one side, and on the other a dynamic relation.

---

[5] Italics are added in this passage, for clarity. The paragraph is quoted in Corrie, *A B C of Jung's Psychology*, pp. 29f.

LECTURE 16

6 July 1925

Dr. Jung:

I think there are some points about the functions in general that need further clarification. I would like to speak now of the four functions in relation to reality, for it is my idea that each of them brings to the subject a special aspect of reality. This diagram then (Diagram 6) represents the four main functions emanating from a virtual center and constituting, in their totality, the subject.

The subject is suspended in a world of objects and cannot be thought of apart from them. Ordinarily we class as objects only those things belonging to the external world, but equally important are the intrapsychical objects with which the subject is in contact. To this latter class belong any conscious content that has slipped out of consciousness, been forgotten, as we say, or repressed, and all unconscious processes. There are always parts of your functions that are within your conscious, and parts that are without your conscious but still within the sphere of psychical activity.

Some of these intrapsychical objects really belong to me, and when I forget them they can be likened to pieces of furniture that have got lost. But some, on the other hand, are intruders into my psychical entourage and come from the collective unconscious. Or the intruder may be from the external world. Take, for example, an institution. This may be unconscious and therefore an object rising out of myself, or it might be started from without by something in the surroundings.

Obviously, the external world does not remain without effect on the functions. If sensations were only subjective and not founded on reality, it would not carry with it the conviction it does. To be sure, not all the sense of conviction rests on the effect derived from the outer object. Sometimes there is also a strong subjective element, as the hallucinations and illusions to be observed in pathological cases prove. But the greater part of the conviction carried by sensation derives from the connection of sensation with the trans-subjective or objective fact in reality. It is of reality as it is that sensation speaks, not reality as it might have been nor as it might be, but as it is *now*. Therefore sensation gives only a static image of reality, and this is the basic principle of the sensation type.

Now, intuition carries with it a similar feeling of certainty, but of a different kind of reality. It speaks of the reality of possibilities, but to an intuitive type this is just as absolute a reality as that possessed by the static fact. Inasmuch as we can test the validity of intuition by seeing whether or not the possibilities do occur actually, and since millions of these possibilities arrived at by intuition have been realized, it is legitimate for the intuitive type to value his function as a means of understanding one phase of reality, that is, dynamic reality.

When we come to the rational functions, things become different. Thinking is based on reality only indirectly, but nonetheless it can carry just as much conviction. Nothing is more real than an idea to a person who thinks. There are certain general or collective ideas from which the thinker derives his judgment, and these we know as the logical modi, but these in turn are derived from some underlying idea; in other words, the logical modi go back to archetypal origins. It would be difficult indeed to trace out their history, but someday, when men are more intelligent than they are now, it will undoubtedly be done. But if we follow the history of thought in the rough way

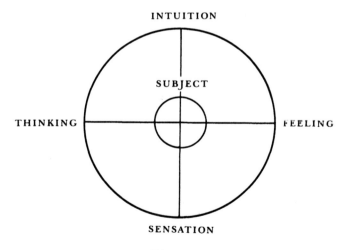

Diagram 6

possible for us, it can be readily seen that all times have recognized the existence of primordial images. To Kant they were the noumena, "das Ding an sich." To Plato they were the eidola, the models that existed before the world existed, and from which all things in the world were derived.

Thinking, then, derives from the reality of the image, but has the image reality? To answer that question, let us turn to the field of natural science, where we can find abundant evidence of the potency of an image. If you cut an earthworm in two, the segment with the head will grow a new tail, and the tail segment will grow a new head. If you destroy the lens of a salamander's eye, a new lens will develop. In both these cases it must be assumed that the organism carries within itself, in some way, an image of its totality, which totality tends to be reestablished when disturbed. In the same way, the fact that the mature oak is contained within the acorn suggests this principle of the image of the whole. Of course, the principle of reestablishing the integrity of the whole when a portion is lopped off works within limitations. The thing replaced is of a more archaic type than the original. So one can say in general that if a differentiated form is removed, the organ substituted goes back to a more primitive level. The same thing happens psychologically. That is, as soon as we set aside the more differentiated function, we hark back to the archaic level. We can see such a thing even in so simple a thing as the progress of an argument. If we fail to convince by means of logical thought, we abandon it and resort to more primitive means, that is, we raise our voices, catch after current phrases, become sarcastic or bitter. In other words, our refined tools failing, we grasp the hammer and tongs of emotion.

Returning to this question of the images, we find something in nature corresponding to the principle involved in them. When we apply the conception to thinking only, we suppose the images to be static. The great philosophers have spoken of them always as being eternal. It is these static images that underlie thinking. We could call them, if we chose, Logos.

Feeling, as we have seen, has also its reality conviction, that is, it has to do with a trans-subjective fact. If we take it from certain aspects, it can bear a resemblance to thinking, but this is merely an apparent, not a real connection. Thus, for example, I can take the concept freedom, and show it to be a highly abstract static concept; that is, I can keep it an idea, but freedom can convey also a powerful feeling. In the same way, the phrase "my country" can be taken abstractly or emotionally. In this way, most of our general ideas are feeling values and intellectual images also, so that we can say that the underlying fact of feeling is a dynamic image. That is to say, it is an image that works, it has motive power. An abstract statement of feeling does not move, it is static. If I define God as the unchanging totality of all changing processes, what have I but a thoroughly static idea? But it is easy to imagine God as a most potently dynamic image. For the totality of the dynamic images can use Eros.

To sum up, we have considered four kinds of realities: (1) static reality that comes to us through sensation; (2) the dynamic reality revealed by intuition; (3) static images given us by thinking; (4) dynamic images sensed by feeling.

I assume that the fact of the discovery of the four functions is equivalent to a statement about the world, that is, that the world has these four aspects of reality. We have no way of knowing whether the world is Cosmos or Chaos, for, as we know the world, all the order is put into it by ourselves. We can think of the possibility of the world changing in such a way as to bring another function, or other functions, into existence; meantime I offer these conceptions as a possible point of orientation.

So now you see what I think of feeling.

I have been asked whether, if a number of individuals in the class draw up a statement of feeling as it appears to them, I would be willing to discuss it. Of course I will do this very gladly, it will be an advantageous way of going into the subject; but I must warn you not to take feeling too subjectively in that case. Each function type has a special way of viewing feeling, and is likely to find things about it which are untrue for the other types. Thus one of the points with respect to the functions that has been most combated is my contention that feeling is rational. My books have been read largely by intellectuals, who have, of course, not been able to see feeling from this aspect, because feeling in themselves is thoroughly irrational by reason of its contamination by elements from the unconscious. Similarly, people with a fairly developed amount of feeling, but in whom there is also intuition with it, hold feeling to be an irrational function.

It is the fate of people to seek to interpret life chiefly through the function strongest in them. Sometimes it is quite impossible to convince a person that he cannot grasp the trans-subjective world with one function alone, no matter how strong that function may be. With respect to the thinking type, this was once borne in upon me very impressively by a man who came to consult me about a compulsion neurosis.[1] He said to me, "I don't think you can cure me, but I would like to know why it is that I can't be cured, because as you will see, there is really nothing that I do not know about myself." And that proved to be true, he had covered his case with truly remarkable intelligence and from the Freudian point of view he was completely analyzed, for there was no corner of his past, even back to the remotest infancy, that remained unexplored. For a moment I could not make out myself why it was that he could not get well. Then I began to question him about his financial situation, as he was just coming from St. Moritz and had spent the winter at Nice. "Were you able to make so much money that you could live that way without working?" I asked him. He became annoyed with me for pressing this point, but finally had to tell the truth, namely that he was unable to work, had never made any money for himself, but was being supported by a schoolteacher, ten years older than himself. He said none of this had anything to do with his neurosis, that he loved the woman, and she him, and they both had *thought* the situation out together and that it was all right. Nor was I ever able to make him see that he was behaving like a pig to this woman, who was living on next to nothing while he was carousing over Europe. He left my office with the firm conviction that, having "thought" the whole thing out, as he was pleased to put it, that finished it.

But the sensation type can crucify reality with equal facility. Suppose there is a woman who has fallen in love with her sister's husband. He is her brother-in-law, and one does not fall in love with one's brother-in-law, therefore the fact is never admitted into consciousness. It is only the facts as they are controlled by the situation as it is that come into the argument; the possibilities behind must be carefully excluded. So these two live for twenty years and only arrive at the true state of affairs through analysis.

I have spoken more than once of the way an intuitive type can neglect reality, and you can, I am sure, supply an equal number of examples of the ways a feeling type can do the same thing. If a thing is disagreeable to the feelings, a feeling type will slide over the reality of it with the greatest facility.

Inasmuch as women are more connected with Eros than are men, they tend to have particular notions about feeling, just as men, even

[1] Jung first described this case, with more detail, in one of the lectures he delivered in London in 1924; see above, Lecture 14, n. 1. Cf. "Analytical Psychology and Education" (CW 17), par. 182; also "Basic Postulates of Analytical Psychology" (1931), CW 8, par. 685, and "The Tavistock Lectures" (1935), CW 18, par. 282.

if not intellectual, tend to have particular notions about thinking. So it is hard for men and women to understand one another. The woman tends to identify feeling with reality, the man clings obstinately to the logical statement.

*

Up to this time we have spoken of the subject as though it were unchanging in time, but as we know, the body is a four-dimensional entity, the fourth dimension being time. If the fourth dimension were spatial, our bodies would be wormlike—that is, drawn out in space between two points. In Diagram 7, I have tried to give some idea of an individual moving through space, that is, three-dimensional space. The individual cannot be understood merely as a static entity. If we want to have a complete notion for the individual, we must add the factor of time. Time means a past and a future, and so the individual

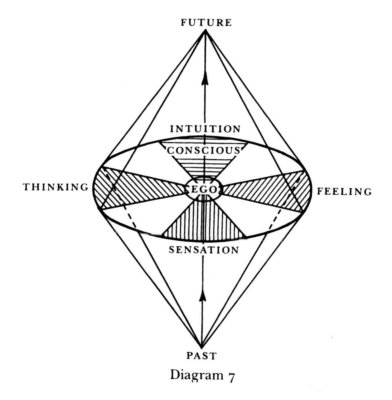

Diagram 7

is only complete when we add his actual structure as the result of past events, and at the same time the actual structure taken as the starting point of new tendencies. According to this idea, we can make out two types, those individuals who hang back in their time under the spell of the past, and others too much ahead of themselves. The latter are only to be understood by their tendencies.

So far, these pictures have disregarded the unconscious. In Diagram 8, I have brought this factor into consideration. This diagram presupposes a fully developed thinking type in whom sensation and intuition are half conscious and half unconscious, and in whom feeling is in the unconscious. This does not mean that such a type is devoid of feeling; it only means that, compared to his thinking, his feeling is not under his control but eruptive in character, so that normally it is not in the picture at all, and then all of a sudden it quite possesses him.

In Diagram 9, I have shown the individual in relation to the world of external objects on the one hand and to the collective unconscious images on the other. Connecting him with the first world, that is, the

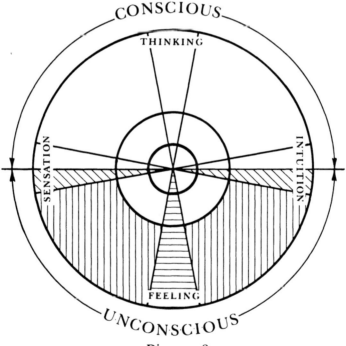

Diagram 8

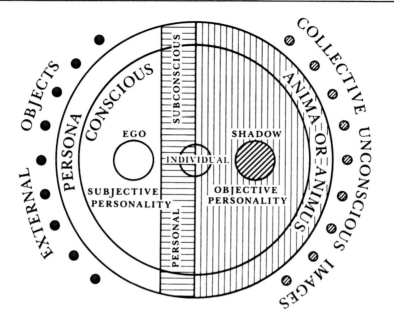

Diagram 9

world of external objects, is the persona, developed by the forces from within and the forces from without in interaction with one another. We may think of the persona as the bark of a conscious personality. As we have indicated elsewhere, it is not wholly our choice what the persona shall be, for we can never control entirely the forces that are to play on our conscious personalities.

The center of this conscious personality is the ego. If we take the layer "back" of this ego, we come to the personal subconscious. This contains our incompatible wishes or fantasies, our childhood influences, repressed sexuality, in a word all those things we refuse to hold in consciousness for one reason or another, or which we lose out of it. In the center is the virtual nucleus or central government, representing the totality of the conscious and unconscious self.

Then we come to the collective unconscious as it is present in us—that is, the part of the racial experience which we carry within us. It is the home of Cabiri or dwarfs whom we may not see else they cease to serve us. In this region another virtual center often turns up in dreams. It is a minor figure of oneself usually projected on a friend, for the unconscious pays these compliments very easily. I have called it the shadow self. The primitive has developed an intricate set of relationships to his shadow which symbolize very well my idea of the shadow self. He must never tread on another's shadow, so too we must never mention the weaknesses of another, those things in him of which he is ashamed and has therefore put out of sight. A primitive says, "Don't go out at midday, it is dangerous not to see your shadow." We say, "Be careful when you don't know your weaknesses."

We can speak of the conscious ego as the subjective personality, and of the shadow self as the objective personality. This latter, made up of what is part of the collective unconscious in us, carries the things that appear in us as effects. For we do have effects on people which we can neither predict nor adequately explain. Instinct warns us to keep away from this racial side of ourselves. If we became aware of the ancestral lives in us, we might disintegrate. An ancestor might take possession of us and ride us to death. The primitive says, "Don't let a ghost get into you." By this he conveys the double idea, "Don't let a visitor get into your unconscious, and don't lose an ancestral soul."

The feeling of awe of the primitive with respect to what we call the collective unconscious is very great. It is to him the ghost world. The following story told by an explorer among the Eskimo is an example of this awe, shared even by the medicine man.[2] The explorer came to the hut of a Polar Eskimo where incantations were going on over a sick man for the purpose of driving away the ghosts or evil spirits that were making him sick. There was a tremendous noise going on, with the sorcerer jumping and running about like mad. As soon as he saw the explorer he became very quiet and said: "This is all a nonsense." He had taken him for another medicine man because no one but a medicine man is supposed to approach a hut where such an incantation is going on. It is the custom, too, for the medicine men who are struggling with the ghosts to smile and say to one another that the whole thing is nonsense, not because they think it is, but because they use it as a sort of apotropaic joke. It is in the nature of a euphemism that should protect them against their own fear.

This instinctive fear of the collective unconscious is very strong indeed in us. There can be a continual flow of fantasies inundating us

[2] Jung's source may have been Knud Rasmussen, *Neue Menschen; ein Jahr bei den nachbarn des Nordpols* (1907), a book that was in his library, or Rasmussen, *Across Arctic America* (1927), which he cited in the *Dream Analysis* seminar, pp. 5f. (1928).

from it, the danger signal coming when the flow cannot be stopped. If one has once seen this happen one feels deeply frightened. We have in general not much imagination about these things, but the primitive knows all about it. For the most part, we are so cut off from it as to float above it.

When it comes to the rather delicate task of locating the collective unconscious, you must not think of it as being compassed by the brain alone but as including the sympathetic nervous system as well. Only that part of it that is your vertebrate inheritance—that is, that comes to you from your vertebrate ancestors—is to be thought of as within the limits of the central nervous system. Otherwise it is outside your psychological sphere. The very primitive animal layers are supposed to be inherited through the sympathetic system, and the relatively later animal layers belonging to the vertebrate series are represented by the cerebrospinal system. The most recent human layers form the basis of actual consciousness, and thus the collective unconscious is reaching into consciousness, and only thus far can you call the collective unconscious psychological. We wish to reserve the term "psychological," used thus, for those elements which, theoretically at least, can be brought into conscious control. On this basis the main body of the collective unconscious cannot be strictly said to be psychological but psychical. We cannot repeat this distinction too often, for when I have referred to the collective unconscious as "outside" our brains, it has been assumed that I meant hanging somewhere in mid-air. After this explanation it will become clear to you that the collective unconscious is always working upon you through trans-subjective facts which are probably inside as well as outside yourselves.

As an example of how the collective unconscious can work upon you through the inside fact, I would give the following: Suppose a man is sitting somewhere out of doors and a bird flies down near him. Another day he is in the same place and a similar bird comes. This time the bird stirs him in an altogether strange way, there is something mysterious attaching to that second bird. The naïve man certainly assumes that the extraordinary effect of the second bird belongs as much to the outside world as the ordinary effect produced by the first bird. If he is a primitive he will distinguish between the two effects by saying the first bird is just a bird, but the second is a "doctor" bird. But we know that the extraordinary effect of the "doctor" bird is due to a projection upon it from the collective unconscious, from within the man.

Ordinarily, it is only by such a projection into the external world that we become conscious of the collective unconscious images. Thus suppose we meet with an extraordinary effect from without. An analysis of that effect shows that it amounts to a projection of an unconscious content, and so we arrive at the realization of such a content. The case mentioned above is an ordinary one insofar as we assume an individual who is chiefly identical with the ego or conscious, but if it should happen that the individual should be more on the side of his shadow, then he would be capable of realizing without projection an immediate—that is, an autonomous—movement of the unconscious contents. But if the individual is identical with his normal ego, then even such an autonomous manifestation of the unconscious—that is, one not released by the projection, nor by external effect, but originating within himself—appears to him as if in the external world. In other words, it requires a very close contact with the unconscious, and an understanding of it, for a man to realize that the origin of his mythological or spiritual experiences is within himself, and that whatever forms these experiences may appear to take, they do not in fact come from the external world.

Using the diagram I have just discussed, that is, Diagram 9, we could give an explanation of analysis. The analyst makes his approach through the persona. Certain formalities of greeting are gone through, and compliments exchanged. In this way, one comes to the gateway of the conscious. Then the conscious contents are carefully examined, and the one passes to the personal subconscious. Here the doctor often marvels that many of the things found there are not conscious since they seem so obvious to an observer. At the personal subconscious a Freudian analysis ends, as I indicated above. When you have finished with the personal subconscious, you have finished with the causal influence of the past. Then you must come to the reconstructive side, and the collective unconscious will speak in images and the consciousness of unconscious objects will begin. If you can succeed in breaking down that dividing wall made by the personal subconscious, the shadow can be united with the ego and the individual becomes a mediator between two worlds. He can now see himself from the "other side" as well as from "this side." Here consciousness of the shadow self is not though,[3] one must have the unconscious images also at one's disposal. The animus or the anima begins to be active now, and the anima will bring in the figure of the old man. All these figures will be projected into the conscious external

[3] The transcript seems to be garbled here. Perhaps "enough."

world, and objects of the unconscious begin to correspond to objects in the external world, so that the latter, the real objects, take on a mythological character. This means an enormous enrichment of life.

*

I have often been asked about the "geology" of a personality, and so I have tried to picture this after a fashion. Diagram 10 shows individuals coming out of a certain common level, like the summits of mountains coming out of a sea. The first connection between certain individuals is that of the family, then comes the clan which unites a number of families, then the nation which unites a still bigger group. After that we could take a large group of connected nations such as would be included under the heading "European man." Going further down, we would come to what we could call the monkey group,

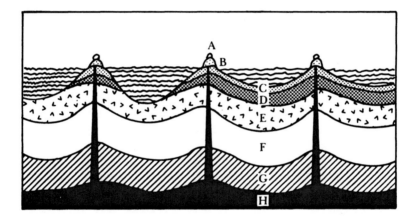

A = Individuals.
B = Families.
C = Clans.
D = Nations.
E = Large Group (European man, for example).
F = Primate Ancestors.
G = Animal Ancestors in general.
H = "Central Fire."

Diagram 10

or that of the primate ancestors, and after that would come the animal layer in general, and finally the central fire, with which as the diagram shows, we are still in connection.[4]

There has apparently been considerable misunderstanding of what I have said about the relation of the subject to the external object, and also about the relation of the subject to the world of the unconscious images. In the supplementary material I have added to the lecture as given in the class, I hope to have been able to clear up these points, but as they are of unusual importance, it is worthwhile to pursue the matter further even if it should take us somewhat far afield. Let us look at the matter historically, in order to get more light on the problem of the relation of the subject to the external object. This is a theme philosophers have been in dispute about from very ancient times. The doctrine of the *esse in re* was the point of view held by the antique world. Everything we perceive outside ourselves is so completely "outside" as to be in no way conditioned by our way of perceiving it. It is even as though there were emanations from our eyes illuminating the object and making it visible to us, so little cognizance does this view take of the subjective side of seeing. This is the notion held by the uneducated man today.

This conception was followed by that of *esse in intellectu solo*; that is, what we see is an image in the head and nothing but that. The question as to whether there are things beyond is left open. This would lead to a solipsism, and makes of the world a gigantic hallucination.

Our idea is of *esse in anima*. This principle recognizes the objectivity of a world outside ourselves, but it holds that of this world we can never perceive anything but the image that is formed in our minds. We never see an object as such, but we see an image which we project out upon the object. We positively know that this image is only imperfectly similar to things as they are. Thus it is indubitable that sound consists of waves; but only when the waves come at a certain rate, let us say sixteen to the second approximately, do we perceive waves as sound. When the vibration is at sixteen or a more rapid rate, we do not sense waves at all, but hear a sound; below that rate we

---

[4] *Footnote in the transcript*: A number of points of confusion having come up in connection with the lecture, Dr. Jung added to the notes supplementary material as well as the appendix which follows.

hear no sound, but feel the vibration of the air on the skin. The same is true of light, which has wave character when examined with suitable apparatuses, but which to our eye has nothing of the kind. That shows in how far the world as we perceive it is a subjective image—that is, an image within us—but at the same time this image is related, and indispensably related, to a thing in itself whose absolute nature is independent of our senses and impossible for us to perceive. Whatever we perceive is an image in the psyche. In that sense, even external reality is in our heads, but only in that sense, and we must avoid speaking too much of the world as subjective images, lest we convey the impression of holding to transcendental idealism, which is practically *esse in intellectu solo*.

The *esse in anima* admits the subjective nature of our world perception, at the same time maintaining the assumption emphatically that the subjective image is the indispensable link between the individual entity, or entity of consciousness, and the unknown strange object. I even hold that this case of the subjective image is the very first manifestation of a sort of transcendent function that derives from the tension between the entity of consciousness and the strange object.

Everything I said about the image of the so-called external reality I have to say also about the images of the collective unconscious: namely, they refer to the influences of absolutely existing external objects, and they are the psychic reactions to them, the only difference between the image of external reality and the archetype being that the former is conscious and the latter unconscious. The archetype nonetheless appears also in the so-called external world if it is not "dug up" in ourselves by an analytical procedure. But you can apply the same analytical processes to the image of external reality also, and see how subjective they are.

There is a further difference between the images of external reality and the archetypes. Images of external reality make up the contents of our conscious memory and also of our artificial reminiscences—that is, our books, archives, etc.—while the archetypes are records of reactions to subjective sense-images. In our conscious memory we record things as they are subjectively, as memories of real facts, but in the unconscious we record the subjective reactions to the facts as we perceive them in the conscious. I should suppose that there are layers even of such repercussions, reactions of reactions, and that they would form the stratification of the mind.

Let us take an example: The fact of Christianity persisting through the ages has left a certain reaction in our unconscious minds; let us call it reaction *b*. This is a repercussion to another reaction we can call reaction *a*, that is, our conscious relation to Christianity throughout the ages. It is reaction *b*, the repercussion to the conscious reaction, which reaches the unconscious strata and persists in our minds as an archetype.

That reaction *b* is modeled on an archetype already, which archetype is simply molded and reshaped by the new deposit. Or to take another example: the most regular recurrence in the world is the rising and the setting of the sun. Our consciousness remembers the real facts of this phenomenon, but our unconscious has recorded the untold millions of sunrises and sunsets in the form of a hero myth, and the hero myth is the expression of the way in which our unconscious has reacted to the conscious image of sunrise and sunset. As reaction *a* is forming the image of the external world, so reaction *b* is forming the collective unconscious—what one could call a sort of mirage world or reflex world.

But it would be somewhat of a depreciation to make the dignity of the collective unconscious one of secondhand origin only. There is another kind of consideration that allows us to envisage the collective unconscious as a firsthand phenomenon, something *sui generis*, in the following way. As we assume that behind our image of the external world there is an absolute entity, so necessarily we must assume that behind the perceiving subject there is an entity; and when we start our consideration from that end, we must say the collective unconscious is reaction *a*, or the first reaction, or first image of the world, while the conscious would be secondhand only.

"SHE"[5]

At the preceding meeting of the class, Mr. Radin presented the story of *She*, together with a sketch of the characters involved. The analysis was postponed till the next meeting, which is recorded here.

Dr. Harding, who gave the analysis, said the committee had decided to treat the book as presenting the material of an anamnesis, and then to take Holly as the conscious side of Haggard, and to analyze Holly through the material given in the story. A very thorough

---

[5] There is no indication whether these reports and discussions took place at the 6 July meeting (as assumed for the present edition) or a subsequent one. For the assignment of the readings, see above, Lecture 15 (one week earlier).

136

analysis was given, of which the following is only an outline summary.

Holly has come to the time of life when he should have settled down to academic life; that is, he is about to give himself up to the absolute one-sidedness of an intellectual. Just then comes the call from the unconscious. All the other sides of life that he has discarded mobilize themselves for a last effort to get his attention. The knock at the door, this stirring of the unconscious, brought an enigmatic thing that could not be touched then, and also a live thing, Leo, who forced him into a new orientation to life. The enigmatic thing lies dormant for twenty years, and then is taken up again. The casket is opened. He consents to consider his unconscious contents, and he goes through them layer by layer, till he comes to the sherd and the scarab. The casket reveals Holly's problem as it has been relived throughout the ages, that is, conventional morality over against the thing that means life.

Holly and Leo, the youthful side of Holly, struggling now to come into being, set out for the land of Kor—that is, Holly will go deeper and deeper into the unconscious until he finds the anima figure, "She," who rules over all the things he has denied admittance into his mind. When "She" is found, and finally loved by Holly, he is for a moment on the verge of madness. He speculates on the possibility of imposing his unconscious symbol upon the external world. That is, can "She" be taken to England?

The innumerable adventures in the land of Kor, all of them important mileposts on the way of Holly's psychological development, culminate in the great test of burning in the pillar of flame. They, Holly and Leo, wisely decide not to risk the test. Holly is not ready for the fundamental change of attitude demanded of him. But he can never again be the commonplace person he started out as; something of the inner meaning of life has been found by him.

*

Dr. Jung: I have to thank the committee and Dr. Harding for their presentation of *She*. They have brought out some brilliant ideas, and I have enjoyed their report very much.

Now I would like to make a few criticisms. Why did you think of Holly as the hero? At any rate, some other views of this point are possible. I think that the author certainly intended Leo as the hero. This fact is brought out with perfect definiteness in the second volume, where Leo, much developed as a personality, is the pivotal character. But of course it is a problem as to whether the author succeeds in his intention in this volume we are discussing, or whether it simply is his viewpoint, and the fact that Dr. Harding has found Holly to be the hero suggests that Haggard has not succeeded.

Dr. Harding: Isn't the point whether Leo is the hero of the story or psychologically the hero?

Dr. Jung: Of course the whole thing is a fantasy of Haggard's, and inasmuch as Haggard has more of himself in Holly probably than in Leo, one might say that Holly is the hero, but nonetheless he is trying to make Leo the hero of the story. Because Haggard is too much Holly in reality, Leo remains a shadowy, relatively undeveloped figure; he has not lived Leo, in other words.

Unfortunately the Tauchnitz edition[6] of *She* does not contain a poem which appears in the English edition, and which really gives a clue to Haggard's relationship to the story. In this poem dedicated to "She," he says that it is not in the land of Kor and it caves, nor in any mysterious land, but in the heart that the grave of the lost love is to be found, and that there dwells "She." This shows what he intended *She* to be. It is a love story, his own love story let us say, but it is not given from the conscious side, but instead from the unconscious side, as a repercussion from the conscious experience, whatever it was. This, of course, is the habit of the introverted writer. So *She* is valuable to us as bringing out these unconscious reactions. The author has evidently had a peculiar love affair which he never quite settled to his satisfaction. It left him with the problem of *She*, and the same problem follows him through most of his books. Perhaps it happened to him in Africa.[7]

We could treat Holly as one unconscious figure and Leo as another, then different aspects of Haggard's character. When you took Holly as the hero, you were not so far from one sense of the book, as we said; since, as we noted, Haggard has identified with Holly. He, like Holly, has probably not seen the importance of his love affair, and when that happens, when a person has an emotional experience and refuses to take it seriously enough, it means a piling up of material in the unconscious. This has been the case with Haggard evidently.

---

[6] The "Collection of British and American Authors," published (in English) by a German firm for sale on the Continent, not legally to be taken into American or British territory.

[7] Sir Henry Rider Haggard (1856–1925) had served in South Africa from 1875 to 1880 as secretary to the governor of Natal before returning to England and marrying an English heiress. His romantic novels brought him fame and fortune.

Now there are a few details I would like to discuss. Have you any idea why this ancient material comes up?

Miss Corrie: It is out of the collective unconscious.

Dr. Jung: Yes, but why does it come up?

Miss Corrie: It always does with introverts sooner or later.

Dr. Jung: No, not necessarily.

Mr. Schmitz: Could not *She* be taken as a revolt on the part of Haggard to the whole Victorian age, and especially to the Victorian woman? Rider Haggard traveled a great deal in foreign countries and was especially well fitted to overthrow the ridiculous idea of a woman that had grown up in England, and to develop the fact that every woman should have some of "She" in her.

Dr. Jung: Part of what you say brings us to the point. That is, if Rider Haggard had not traveled in primitive countries, the collective unconscious would not have been activated in the peculiar way it was. It would not have been so dynamic in its reaction. Of course, there is another way in which the collective unconscious can be strongly stimulated. A man has had a psychosis, there has been formed a hole in his unconscious so to speak, and there is always a chance of the collective breaking through. But that was not the case with Haggard, his unconscious was animated by contact with the primitive life about him. It is very interesting indeed to observe the effect of life in primitive countries upon civilized men coming to them. It is said of many of the officials that return to England from India that they come home with burned brains. But of course it has nothing to do with the climate. Their vitality has simply been sucked away in that alien atmosphere. These men try to keep up the standards to which they have been trained, in a country where everything is set in the opposite direction, and the strain breaks them.

I have treated several cases of men returning from the colonies after long association with native women. They cannot love European women after this experience. They come with all sorts of symptoms, of indigestion, etc., but in reality they have been dissociated by the native women. A primitive would say they have lost a soul. There is a very good story illustrating this in an otherwise very poor book by Algernon Blackwood. The book is called *Incredible Adventures*,[8] and the story is "Descent into Egypt." The man simply fades out, he is gone as a European.

---

[8] London, 1914. Blackwood (1869–1951) wrote many short stories on supernatural themes. His work has been compared to that of Gustav Meyrink.

This then is the reason for the tremendous welling up of the collective unconscious in Rider Haggard. The fact that it comes about through his contact with the primitive complicates the love problem. But how could his love problem be complicated by the fact of his life in Africa?

Mr. Schmitz: Perhaps "She" is such a complete opposite to the women of Dickens, let us say, that she can be taken as a wish-fulfillment. Of course he would not want such a woman as "She," and yet he would understand that in part "She" is necessary; that is, that a woman must have a primitive side in order to be complete, just as in the case of a man.

Dr. Jung: But if he had such an idea of what a woman ought to be, it should have helped him in his problem.

Mr. Schmitz: He was not clear about it, so the unconscious produced this desire.

Dr. Jung: It is out of this groping about in his unconscious that *She* developed. But why should a man in Africa be less able to handle a love problem?

Mr. Robertson: Isn't it because the African situation makes it hard for him to handle his feelings in the old way?

Dr. Jung: Yes, if you don't look at it in too special a way, it could be put in those terms. That is, the man's attitude toward the love problem changes, and it becomes really a terrible problem for him.

Mr. Bacon: Does not the problem consist in his projecting a primitive anima on a non-primitive woman?

Dr. Jung: Yes, that is exactly it, and when that happens, the non-primitive woman becomes perfectly hysterical under it.

The whole problem of the projection of the anima is a most difficult subject. If a man cannot project his anima, then he is cut off from women. It is true he may make a thoroughly respectable marriage, but the spark of fire is not there, he does not get complete reality into his life.

Coming back now to the story: how do you understand the father of Leo?

Dr. Harding: Except as one of the former heroes in the legend, we did not attempt to interpret him.

Dr. Jung: He is certainly not a strong character, in fact he is just fading out when the story begins. But that is important in itself, for psychologically we know the father must fade when the hero comes, otherwise the development of the hero is seriously hindered. I mention this because it is of great importance in the Egyptian religion around which this fantasy of Haggard's plays. Thus Osiris fades into a ghost who rules over the dead, and his son Horus becomes the rising sun. It is an eternal theme.

Mr. Schmitz: An excellent example of the need of the son for having the father out of his way before he can come into his own is seen in the case of Frederick the Great, who was markedly effeminate up to the very day of his father's death. Kubin,[9] too, never wrote at all until after his father died.

Dr. Jung: It is truly a critical moment in a man's life. Often instead of being released for life by the death of the father, the son becomes neurotic. Mythology takes note of the fact that it is so critical a moment; in fact, all these great moments of life have been embodied in mythology, because the latter sets forth the average solution found by humanity in its problems.

I think you have interpreted the chest quite properly. The fact that there is a chest within a chest suggests a process of involution.

When it comes to the love of Kallicrates,[10] we find the whole story anticipated in remotest times. Why is that so?

Dr. Bertine: It is because it is not an individual story but repeats an archetypal pattern.

Dr. Jung: Quite so. It is an eternal truth. It says that man is to play this role over and over again. This is another cause for the coming up of the unconscious material. But which archetype is it that is reawakened?

It is the myth of Osiris, Isis, and Nephthys. The myth says that Osiris was in the womb of his mother Nut together with Isis the queen of the day and Nephthys the queen of night, and while in the womb he had sexual intercourse with his two sisters. Here is an everrecurring motive, the conflict between the two for the love of the hero. Therefore we have the conflict between "She" and Amenartis. In the *Return of She*[11] the conflict comes up again, this time between "She" and the Tartar queen who wants to marry Leo. Again it is the conflict between day and night, only this time "She" impersonates Isis, and the other is Nephthys. This is the archetype aroused in Haggard by Africa. Haggard was a thoroughly "respectable" man and no doubt his marriage a thoroughly conventional one, but one can read

[9] The Expressionist artist and writer Alfred Kubin was married to Schmitz's sister. Jung cited his novel *Die andere Seite* (1909) as "a classic example of the direct perception of unconscious processes" (*Jung: Letters*, vol. 1, p. 104: 19 Nov. 1932).

[10] Kallicrates: not the Greek architect of the 5th century B.C., but a figure in *She*.

[11] Haggard, *Ayesha, or the Return of She* (1895).

between the lines of *She* that he loved another woman in all probability.

Who is Leo in the author? Holly is relatively an old man, he has come into the age of wisdom where he is really too old to take on the risks the problem involves. Therefore he creates the youthful figure of Leo. The latter is hardly more than a youthful fool, but he is altogether a gentleman. Through his youth he compensates the old Holly and allows the latter to play safe. It is always Leo that takes the risks even to the point of being almost hot-potted.

Do you know what is the significance of hot-potting?

Mr. Schmitz: I should think it would mean the heat of the passions taking the head.

Dr. Jung: And what does that mean? Insanity—all over the place, as the saying is. I have scarcely seen anyone who did not have that reaction to the collective unconscious. At first the past looks dead, but as we get closer it gets us. Take for example an old house. One is at first so delighted at its antiquity, and then little by little an atmosphere of mystery gathers about it, and then before we know it, we have "ghosts" on our hands. Something about the house has activated the unconscious in us. Just give a little libido to it and the collective unconscious takes on an enormous attraction for us. Just look at the power of history over our minds as another example.

Mr. Radin: Walter Scott is a case of the past swallowing a man's conscious adaptation, for when he moved into Abbotsford and began to live into history, so to speak, he lost all his money, and all power of directing his life.[12]

Miss Corrie: "She" said her kingdom was of the imagination.

Dr. Jung: Yes, when you give yourself to the imagination, you are in effect lost to this world. Soon you can no longer explain yourself and then the way to the lunatic asylum is clear. That is why, when the collective unconscious is near, one must learn some form of expression so as to create a bridge to reality. Otherwise there is nothing to hold to, and the individual is a prey to the forces released. When people are lost in the collective and you can provide a form in which they can cast their ideas, they can come over into sanity again.

That, then, is the danger in hot-potting. It is done by the primitive. The primitive layers are so thick they can easily overcome you.

I think your interpretation of Job the correct one—that is, the com-

---

[12] Scott purchased his estate, Abbotsford, in 1811; published the first of the Waverley novels in 1814; and suffered financial ruin in 1826.

monplace, correct man happily gets lost. This amounts to saying that Holly can never be a don again. Offsetting the loss of Job is Leo's receiving the cloak of "She." Leo gets into shape, he receives something from "She" but only after Holly gives up his conventional aspect, i.e., Job.

You said nothing about Ustane.

Dr. Harding: That was because there was already too much to be said, and she seemed relatively unimportant.

Dr. Jung: Yes, she was in fact dead.

I think you have got Noot, Billali, and Holly rightly placed, that is, as figures of the wise old man. Holly is the most human of them. Haggard is inclined to identify himself with the wise old man through Holly, but there is more of pedantry than real wisdom in the figure of Holly. It is rather typical that Holly should have explored the graves while Leo was about to die.

You spoke of a passage about a unicorn and a goose, where was that?

Dr. Harding: No, not a unicorn, but a goose that was shot after the fight between the Lion and the Crocodile. The goose had a spur on its head and I said it associated to the unicorn.

Dr. Jung: The killing of the goose is surely the same motive as that in the Grail story, as you indicated. It is an omen or presage of coming events. The ancients always thought of coming events as having shadows cast in front of them. Here we have an animal killed, a mythological animal in fact—that is, instinct. When it is killed, someone will become conscious. In the story of Parcival,[13] the unconscious hero Parcival becomes conscious through the shooting of the swan. In *She* the heroes awake to a realization of the extraordinary things ahead of them. A bird is a mind animal, symbolically, so the unconsciousness is in the mind.

One word more on the theme of immortality. It is intimately linked

---

[13] Percivale, Parzival, or Parsifal, the hero of the Grail quest in Arthurian legend, would have been familiar to Jung through the Wolfram von Eschenbach poem and Wagner's opera, both of which he variously cited. (Jung alluded to Parsifal in a letter to Freud, Dec. 1908, 117 J, and mentioned the Grail in *Wandlungen und Symbole*, 1912; cf. *Psychology of the Unconscious*, ch. 6, n. 36, and CW 5, par. 150, nn. 577, 60. Cf. also *Types*, CW 6, par. 371ff.) Apparently Emma Jung began her study of the Grail legend in the year the present seminar took place: cf. Marie-Louise von Franz, foreword (p. 7) to the work left unfinished at Mrs. Jung's death, in 1955, and completed by von Franz, *The Grail Legend* (orig. 1960; tr. Andrea Dykes, New York and London, 1971). According to von Franz, Jung did not undertake research on the connections between the Grail legend and alchemy in deference to his wife's interest.

up with the anima question. Through the relation to the anima one obtains the chance of greater consciousness. It leads to a realization of the self as the totality of the conscious and the unconscious functions. This realization brings with it a recognition of the inherited plus the new units that go to make up the self. That is to say, when we once grasp the meaning of the conscious and the unconscious together, we become aware of the ancestral lives that have gone into the making of our own lives.

You will then come into a realization not only of your human pre-stages, but of the animal also. This feeling of the collective unconscious brings with it a sense of the renewal of life to which there is no end. It comes down from the dim dawn of the world, and continues. So when we obtain a complete realization of self, there comes with it the feeling of immortality. Even in analysis such a moment may come. It is the goal of individuation to reach the sense of the continuation of one's life through the ages. It gives one a feeling of eternity on this earth.

As Dr. Harding pointed out, these men are not ready for the pillar of fire. The whole phenomenon of "She" has not yet been assimilated, the task is still before them, and they must have a new contact with the unconscious.

"THE EVIL VINEYARD"

Dr. Mann gave the report for the committee on *The Evil Vineyard*. Only her synopsis of the psychological aspects of the story will be given. Taken on the reality basis, the story tells of a marriage in which no possibility of a real relationship existed. The girl, having repressed her instincts as a woman, marries Latimer because he stands for the intellectual world which has completely fascinated her. She has no love for him, even fears him. Latimer, twenty years her senior, seeks in her a renewal of youth; instead of feeling, he brings her sexuality. The weirdness he is described as having [experienced] before his marriage progresses through shell shock into a neurosis in which he has to relive the crimes of a legendary Italian condottiere.

Because he represents her projected unconscious, and is in short an animus figure to her, Mary is utterly powerless to free herself from him until she comes to love another man in a real way.

Taken symbolically, the story is that of a woman giving way to the evil side of the animus, finally to be rescued by the upcoming of the positive side. Throughout, Mary was taken as psychologically identical with the author.

It was the opinion of Dr. Jung that the committee had failed to get at the deeper psychological significance of the book, and that the reason that they had failed lay in the assumption that Latimer was abnormal when he met Mary. There was not sufficient evidence, he thought, for that viewpoint, and taking the story that way limited it too much. It should be taken on a much deeper level.

Dr. Jung: I would like to hear from the men on the committee. Mr. Bacon?

Mr. Bacon: The thing that interested me was that I thought if I could have read the symbols rightly, which I did not feel competent to do, I could have learned something very interesting about the author. I thought she must have had some bad experience, and that the book was a reflection of her private troubles.

Dr. Jung: I think it would be a mistake to take the book as too much a story of the author. We really don't know in how far the author has come to it from inner motives, and how much she has taken over the legend of the Casa di Ferro.[14] She seems to have lived in Switzerland and to have known much of Swiss life. In case she has taken over the plot ready-made, it would not be fair to say it is symptomatic. So I think we can dismiss the intuitions about the author's conflict. It was more possible to take *She* from that viewpoint, but here the connections are very obscure. It would be better to take this story from the standpoint of the heroes, as Dr. Harding has done with Holly. Thus I should analyze it first from the standpoint of the girl, and then from that of Latimer. Looked at from the two aspects, very different things come out. We have no book that I know of in which we could establish a direct relationship between the author and the animus figure. But here an important part of the problem is presented. We can assume that the author has put feminine psychology into the heroine, and we can try to reconstruct what that woman has experienced and the development of the animus.

Do you consider, Dr. Mann, that Latimer is a suitable animus figure?

Dr. Mann: Yes, because he is a power figure.

Dr. Jung: I think it nearer the facts to say that he became a power

[14] The 15th-cent. Castello di Ferro, as it is usually called, is in Minusio, on the outskirts of Locarno, on the shore of Lake Maggiore. Cf. *Kunstdenkmaler der Schweiz*, vol. 73 (Basel, 1983), pp. 219ff.

figure. First he appears as a learned man who appealed to her as a source of wisdom, a man representing wisdom. The animus is not necessarily a power figure. The *anima*, on the other hand, is usually a power figure. She appears in that way from the very beginning.

But the response of a woman to wisdom is not necessarily a power reaction, as you seem to have presented it. It is quite a legitimate craving. I think the author has tried to show here a girl who was starved on the spiritual side, and came to an older man legitimately seeking. Of course the world always takes such a situation and makes a love story of it, not allowing that a girl comes to a man for anything but love. When such a thing happens to a man in reality, he is very likely to make the false assumption; and obviously there are more cases in which the assumption is right than those in which it is wrong, but nonetheless, we must admit that there are plenty of serious cases in which a girl can be interested in learning. And so I think Mary sought information from Latimer.

Then begins the tragic situation. He would not assume that she is interested in knowledge, but takes it that she wants him as a man, and is simply pretending an interest in order to trap him. Here is the tragic conflict. He does not see that she is really interested, and so he gets her into a trap. Then comes her mistake. She is not aware of her instincts, and has no love for him whatsoever. It would be her duty to tell him that he has made a mistake, but she just lets him marry her, and never tells him that she does not love him.

Because she has disregarded her instincts, they begin to grow in the dark. Then the animus begins his work, and from this moment he gives an evil twist to her unconscious processes. Before she was all right, and she had projected her animus into Latimer at sight. It was something that simply happened, and if the situation had been taken seriously, it might have gone very well. But his attitude to her was all wrong because it was blind. He took no cognizance of what she really thought about him, and made the false assumption about her seeking him as a lover. A man thoroughly aware of his own instincts should not make a mistake like that, but obviously he was a very intellectual man living in his mind with complete repression of the anima. When he meets her all of that goes over on her, and he never stops to make out the reality of the situation. But she will not carry his projection, and presently he begins to feel something growing in her which he does not understand. And there we are launched upon the battle between the anima and the animus.

Let us take up her side of the conflict first. She committed a sin of ignorance in that she was unaware of her instincts. Nature pays no attention to ignorance as an excuse, she simply punishes it as a sin. She handles the situation as it is, and it makes no difference to nature if the person has chosen the wrong way with malice aforethought, or has merely fallen into it. We might say that ignorance of instinct on the part of Mary is a sort of inherited sin, for her whole education has been along the lines of excluding knowledge of life. Her family did all they could to keep her unconscious, and she knows nothing of the role a woman must play. She quite innocently lies to the man, then she behaves as though she were his wife and really is not.

In such a marriage there will be a violent outburst of sexuality at the beginning on the part of the man. The primitive in the man is awakened because he must beat the woman down in order to make her serviceable to his instincts. Of course this is quite wrong, hopelessly wrong, but he is driven to it, and any natural man will do it. The woman gets into the position of the archaic woman, and then the animal lust of the man is stirred. Negresses in certain parts of Africa exhibit with pride the scars they have received in their sexual battles with men. Then the man is fairly launched on a course of brutality. But an educated man cannot keep this up indefinitely. It breaks him and he becomes impotent.

As long as the woman can be kept down, she is alive as an animal; she becomes the victim of a brute, and takes a certain animal satisfaction out of it. But she cannot keep on that low level any more than the man, and so it leads into a breakdown.

What happens then? The libido with no outlet goes into the unconscious in a lump, one might say. It becomes an egg that she broods over and hatches out. What is in this egg? Feminine instinctiveness. Fantasies begin to form around the figure of a young man who will come and free her from this tyrant. The fantasies go on further and further with this theme of her being a prisoner of a cruel tyrant. Often I have seen this fantasy material about the young man, and the old man who has put the little bird into a gilded cage.

She is indulging in these fantasies, and brooding and brooding, but without knowing why. Hardly any woman in this condition is conscious. Perhaps after she gets to be forty or forty-five she can wake up and know what is happening in her mind, but ordinarily she remains profoundly ignorant of it all. So then we have the formation of these unconscious sexual fantasies; and they make wonderful material out of which an unconscious complex can form. This begins in the personal unconscious. At her first sexual experience she could have understood. Many women do come into consciousness in this way. But when brutal sexuality comes, the deeper layers of the personality are opened up. This leads right back to the monkey age. The libido leaves the surface and goes down into the depths.

When a woman gets to this point she will begin to use historical material in which to wrap the fantasies. Instead of saying "My husband has forced me," she will begin a story of ancient times in which this tragedy was enacted. This historical element points to the collective unconscious. Then it must be determined why it chooses the specific period it does, in this case the Middle Ages. And in this case, it is because the special psychology involved lies within the viewpoint of the Middle Ages. If one goes back, on the other hand, in search of the place in history where the repression of the anima begins, one is taken far beyond the Middle Ages, back of Christianity to paganism. This is far too intricate a theme for me to enter upon here, but it is my belief that the repression of the anima is connected with the problem of the collective domestication of man. In order that the state be made, the anima had to be repressed. That is why the story of Kallicrates in *She* is staged first in ancient times. Not so early as Babylon or Egypt, however, because neither of these countries ever knew a state, strictly speaking. The king was on the level of the gods, as is witnessed by the Babylonian temples; at one end is the king, at the other the god. In some of the Egyptian sculpture, the king is pictured issuing orders to the gods. Of course a state is not possible in such a condition, it is simply the ruling of the herd by the terror of mana. In the Greek *polis*, no such thing existed, and it is there we find the beginning of the state. But if the anima ruled, the formation of a state would be impossible. But how does the repression gradually come about? You have contracts, you promise not to fight under such and such conditions, you put down your weapons and don't speak very loud, you are very polite, you don't tread on another man's shadow. So it goes among primitives, and in this way tolerance has a chance to grow. Through these observances, man's anima became repressed.

In this case the cause of the repression of the instincts lay in medieval psychology, and we must look back into medieval times to find out why. Have you any ideas on this subject?

Mr. Schmitz: Did the repression of the instincts in women not grow out of the man's desire to keep the woman chaste while he went to war?

Dr. Jung: Yes, but you must explain the exaggerated ideal of chastity in these times.

Mr. Schmitz: If one goes as far back as the matriarchy, there is no ideal of chastity in women; but when gradually the patriarchy came about, men became interested in establishing their children's paternity, and so grew up the conception of the chaste wife, and from that they passed to the idea of the virgin powerful through chastity, such as Athena.

Dr. Jung: You make then a connection between the cult of the virgin and the exaggerated idea of chastity. I quite agree with that. This cult brought with it very brutal means of enforcing the chastity. If you go back to primitive tribes, even when a more or less strict monogamy is the rule, it is taken for granted that women are unreliable when the man turns his back, but not too much notice is taken of it unless the man is greatly attached to his wife. It is understood that a woman is not exactly true, but the primitive husband does not particularly care. Nor does the woman on her side mind having the husband go with other women as long as he is not taken from her. In other words jealousy is not so much present. With the ideal of chastity comes jealousy.

Mr. Bacon: Among the natives of Nicaragua,[15] the husband is inordinately jealous of his wife; in fact he becomes quite ferocious about it.

Dr. Jung: Yes, there are certain tribal ideas that explain particular cases, but when you study the average case you will find what I have said to be true. But there are other examples where terrible punishments follow infidelity. Our exaggerated feeling about chastity has brought similar cruelties with it. Primitive punishments are often of a peculiar ferocity, as is shown in the practices surrounding witch-hunting. But what about our own laws in respect to that? In the year 700, the burning of witches was not allowed, but 700 years later, down to 1796, witches were burned. It had its climax at the same time as the appearance of the Lauretanian Litany,[16] which expresses the culmination of the cult of the Virgin. When such cruelties as witch-burning appear in society, it means on the psychological side that instinct has been tortured, and in fact instinct is tortured by an extreme over-valuation of chastity. Really hellish tortures have followed in its wake.

So these medieval fantasies in this book are to be explained by the fact of the complete repression of instinct. Images of times when such

[15] Bacon in his youth had lived in Nicaragua; see his autobiography, *Semi-centennial* (New York, 1939).

[16] Also called the Litany of Loreto (16th cent.). For the text and analysis, cf. *Types* (CW 6), pars. 379, 390ff., 406.

deeds as those of Henrico von Brunnen were generally current are reawakened. As the murderer of his wife and her lover, he forms a suitable figure for the unconscious fantasy material of Mary, who thinks of herself as the prisoner of an ogre. Now, when such fantasies are forming, they permeate the mind, and the collective unconscious is animated and one reacts to it—I mean anyone intimately associated with such a person. It is just as though the animated collective unconscious were sending out waves influencing others. The husband in this story responds to the activation of the collective unconscious in his wife. He is gripped by something he does not understand, and as he becomes restless, he is chased by these collective fantasies of his wife. He does not know where they belong. On his wanderings he comes upon this place, the Casa di Ferro. I know the place, and it is in fact very extraordinary; one wonders what it was, and feels the truth of the legends about it.

When Latimer saw it, something happened to him. He said to himself: "This is the place, and I am that man Henrico von Brunnen." There is the immediate conviction that always follows when an archetype is struck, it is an extraordinary experience. If the fantasy of your partner gets into you, you make yourself responsible for it; and if you hit upon the reality that frames the fantasy, you do just as Latimer did when he said, "I am Henrico von Brunnen—that is my form." This brought him peace, but at the same time he had to live the thing. He fell under the spell of the fantasy and was overcome by it. He was no longer himself, but his unconscious. So he died when he committed the murder. He had not done it himself, nature had brought it about.

To sum up, we see in this story the complete projection of the woman's unconscious into the man, the operation of the animus. Then comes the tragic denial of love. All of the repressed instinctive libido activates the deeper layers of the unconscious with the resulting fantasy system we have seen, till the man upon whom it is projected [falls] under its spell and lives it out. That is the story as determined by the woman's part in it. If we look at it from the man's side it becomes different.

Until his marriage Latimer has lived the life of a learned man. He has repressed the anima completely. Then he goes out to seek "She," and finds her in this lovely young girl. The feeling of youth was stirred in him. He found this girl uncannily unconscious, full of a strange vagueness, and unaware of the instincts as she was, and she became for him a wonderful opportunity for anima projection. Into such a vague, ambiguous frame you can put any amount of fantasy, and so he made a plaything of her. She fulfilled his wish by keeping quiet. The vaguer she became, the more the anima had a chance to play her role. The more she fits into the anima role, the less he can get at her in reality. Then he begins to make assumptions to take the place of the realities. He gets into a complete mist about her, and she becomes more elusive than moonlight. She had denied love, and so he began to seek for this thing he could not find. He began going all over Europe in quest of this unknown thing. Inasmuch as she withdrew all libido from him and began to weave fantasies of lovers who would release her from him, his wife was really untrue to him. He became convinced that she was untrue to him in point of fact, and began to make sure against lovers in the night. Thus following up the suspicions of the anima, he fell deeper and deeper into the snare. Finally he resorted to locking her up. All of these things he was driven to do in order to get rid of the torture that was tearing him to pieces.

Dr. de Angulo: I can see the truth of all that you have said if you take it that Latimer was a normal man when he married Mary, but is there not a justification for taking it as the committee did, that is, that Latimer was already split apart, and abnormal through his one-sidedness when he first met her? His experiences in the war swamped him completely, and then be began to live his unconscious, which finally led to his identification with Henrico von Brunnen. Mary is then only an incident in his life; what drives him to insanity is his inability to get at his feelings. Just because he is so unreal when she meets him, he is an animus figure for Mary.

Dr. Jung: No, I see no justification for assuming that Latimer was abnormal from the beginning. Besides, it is only a hiding behind words to say that, for it does not explain anything.

"L'ATLANTIDE"

Mr. Bacon read the report of the committee on *L'Atlantide*. The committee were of divided opinions as to the proper psychological interpretation. One view was that the book demonstrated a conflict in Benoît's mind between his spiritual side and a tendency toward material considerations. It was felt, for example, that he was conscious of misusing the messages of the unconscious for the sake of writing "bestsellers." Looked at from that angle, Antinéa was not accepted as a true anima figure—that is, a creation of unconscious fantasies—but was taken as having been more than half constructed with a view to literary effect.

Another view represented in the committee was that the book represented a conflict between what was rational and what was irrational in Benoît's psychology, rather than as a conflict between a spiritual and a materialistic viewpoint.

Mr. Aldrich, differing from both of these viewpoints, presented a minority report in which he valiantly defended Antinéa not only as a true anima figure, but also as being a symbol of positive importance. According to his view, Antinéa was neither a good woman nor an evil one, but complete on all sides. He has summarized his report as follows:

"The natural complement of a complete woman is a complete man. Insofar as the man is incompletely developed, or refuses to give her more than one side of his nature, he may expect that she will punish him. In Benoît's romance, the hero is split in two: the sensual side of him is personified by Saint-Avit, while Morhange stands for an infantile and conventional sort of spirituality. In effect, the hero goes to Antinéa and says, 'I tender you my sensual side, because Nature drives me; but I mean to deny you any participation in my spiritual side because, according to my conventional morality, love of woman and spirituality are opposites and cannot be reconciled.' Naturally, this aroused a devil in Antinéa—as it would in any woman who had any individuality. Obviously the right woman for a man is the woman who complements his own stage of development: the mother is suitable for the baby, the wife for the man who is winning his place in the world, and the hetaira—the completely developed woman, the comrade—for the man who has achieved complete individuality, the Wise Man. Antinéa would have been a delightful comrade for a Wise Man; but for a man who had not passed out of the Warrior stage she was as inappropriate and fatal as a wife would be for a baby."

*

Dr. Jung: The most interesting point about this book is the way in which it differs from *She*, is it not, Mr. Bacon?

Mr. Bacon: Yes, I must say I was a little confused in trying to get at the differences, but for one thing there is the theme of luxury greatly emphasized in Benoît's book.

Miss Raevsky: Not only that, there is a sensualism that is much developed in it, even in Antinéa.

Dr. Jung: Yes, if you think of the outside details, there is a tremendous difference. In *L'Atlantide* as you say, there is an atmosphere of luxury, the beauty of the place is dwelt upon, the way which the people are received is described so as to bring out the details, while the corresponding features in *She* are very sparsely treated. Benoît is outspokenly esthetical. One could [not?] imagine an Anglo-Saxon writer paying as much attention to these physical details. Haggard pays a good deal of attention to them himself, in fact, as for example when he describes an afternoon tea under perfectly absurd conditions, but when Haggard does this, it is with a sort of frugality; it is the sort of sensuality that belongs to the sportsman, while Benoît's is that of the salon.

When you mention the sensuality in *L'Atlantide*, you have something, but there is a still greater difference. Benoît fully acknowledges the place of sexuality, while in Haggard it always appears as a fiendish element. In Benoît it plays a big part, while in all of Haggard's books it is decidedly in the background. One could say that one had here the French and the Anglo-Saxon viewpoints in opposition. We cannot assume that the Anglo-Saxon view is the only one in harmony with Heaven; we must assume that the French view has also justification. So it is worthwhile to go into some detail about this question of attitude. In order to do that we must pay some attention to Antinéa. I am not sure if the class got a very clear picture of Antinéa. Mr. Bacon, will you describe the ways in which Antinéa differs from "She"?

Mr. Bacon: Antinéa is a much more physiological object than "She," who is very nebulous. Antinéa is represented as full of animal desire.

Mr. Aldrich: "She" says nothing to me, while Antinéa is to me a real woman. I think I was the only member of the committee who did not think of her as poison. If the author could only have got himself together and not approached her as a split personality, he would have found Antinéa a very nice girl.

Dr. Jung: But you must admit it is a bit of a bad joke to have a salon full of dead men.

Mr. Aldrich: Ah, but she gave them immortality.

Dr. Jung: I must say that view is a little too optimistic, but it is true that Antinéa[17] is usually depreciated, unnecessarily so if her circumstances are taken into consideration. She is an omnipotent queen who can have her every mood and whim satisfied. Such an Oriental queen

[17] *Transcript:* "Atlantide."

can be very cruel without being vicious. If we compare her with other similar types, she is not so bad. Moreover, she is in a difficult situation. She is a woman who has not been hampered by interferences of education; she could unfold quite completely, but we should not assume that this is the best thing that can happen. She sees and appreciates natural values, and she is intelligent and educated intellectually, but she has had no education in the higher values. One can be doubtful, of course, about whether or not these higher values are worthwhile, but it would be a mistake to think they can be utterly neglected. If we compare "She" with Antinéa, we can see that the tragedy hangs about this matter of values. "She" is tortured for thousands of years till she admits them. Antinéa is not even so far along that she admits or sees their existence, and so she does not fight, and we see that Antinéa is on a lower level than "She." Our sympathy therefore goes to the latter. But Antinéa has all the charm of the native woman, all the erotic power and instinctiveness that goes with such a woman. This is somewhat gone in "She," for "She" is already under the influence of things.

But we must remember that Antinéa is not a real woman, but the anima of a Frenchman, and here we have a typical difference between the French and the Anglo-Saxons. If ever there was a book that could throw light on this difference it is this one. I should like to hear from you on this point. How do you explain this peculiar difference?

Mr. Schmitz: I believe that the difference between the French and the Anglo-Saxons, between the French and the rest of Europe for that matter, arises out of the difference in their relation to the pagan world. The French are the only people having a direct connection with this world. When the Romans conquered Gaul they surrounded it with Roman culture. So when Christianity came, it found France a civilized state in contradistinction to Germany. The Germans resisted Roman culture, so there is no continuity of tradition with the pagan world. Christianity found us barbaric, and our paganism has remained with the barbaric element in it. This difference runs through the whole French culture.

Dr. Jung: What Mr. Schmitz says is very true. Therein lies the reason for the difference between the French and the Anglo-Saxon viewpoints. Gaul was civilized in early times; it even contained a fertile Roman culture at a time when Germany and the Anglo-Saxon were in a most primitive state of development. In those days even Paris was in existence as a civilized place, and there were poets, even emperors, coming from the natives of Gaul. It was, in other words, a rich civilization, the old Gauls having been assimilated into the Roman people. The Celtic languages disappeared, and the Germanic tribes that came in were absorbed by the Romanized population and so received the Roman civilization also. On that basis Christianity was planted, not on a wild people as in Germany. Therefore there is an absolute continuity between the Roman mentality and that of the Middle Ages. There is no break. Even certain early Church Fathers were French.

Besides the Roman, there was a strong Greek influence that reached up the Rhone, and cultural influences from the Mediterranean came at a very early date. All of these influences from the pagan world had a peculiar effect. They fortified the antique layers to such an extent that Christianity could not undo it. The same is true more or less for all the Mediterranean peoples; that is, they remained more pagan than Christian. It would be hard to say this to a Frenchman, because the French think of themselves as good Catholics. And so they are, in one sense; even when most skeptical they are still good Catholics. Otherwise Voltaire and Diderot would not be as acceptable as they are. Thus one can be Catholic in a negative way, and be pleased with venom against the thing formerly most reverenced.

Those within the Church have a most positive attitude. They center about Catholicism because they feel it embraces life. Within its scope paganism persists, and so one finds among the most religious Frenchmen a full recognition of sexuality. Today their point of view about sexuality is that it is amoral.[18] It is just obvious that it is accepted, and morality scarcely enters into the question. A man goes regularly to church and keeps up whatever sexual practices he may see fit, for sexuality in his eyes has nothing to do with morality. That is why sexuality receives the special treatment it does in France.

This peculiar difference explains, I think, every difference between "She" and Antinéa. And since Antinéa has so definite a character, we can reconstruct something of the author's conscious and arrive at an appreciation of a modern Frenchman.

Then there are other figures that throw much light on French psychology. Take Le Mesge, for example. Here is a pure rationalist living in an altogether irrational way, a thing typical of the French. It is characteristic of the French mind to allow the limit of irrationality in

[18] *Transcript*: "a moral."

155

behavior, and nowhere else can one see so many comical figures in reality; but they are nonetheless rational in their viewpoints.

Then Count Bielowsky, in spite of being a Pole, is a typical French figure of the Third Empire, a habitué of Paris. His figure forms a necessary counterpart to that of Morhange, whose flirtatious attitude toward the church is compensated by Bielowsky's flirtatious attitude toward "high life." The mediating figure between the two is Le Mesge. Such contradictions always demand a compromise, and this comes about through a rational mediation. But here there is too little life, so then Saint-Avit is brought in to provide temperament and passion.

A Frenchman always allows himself to have "fits," where he can apply a whole arsenal of rhetoric. There comes out a long series of tremendous words, put together in a perfect style, and then he is all right.

Mr. Aldrich: Morhange, according to the way I see him, has only a very feeble spirituality. I don't believe he ever had a religious emotion.

Dr. Jung: But you are Anglo-Saxon and he was a Catholic. We can never know what Sacré-Cœur[19] means to them, nor how they can excite themselves over the image of the Virgin.

We can say then that there is a peculiar atmosphere in *L'Atlantide*, and an altogether different one from *She*. This is something I felt very profoundly and wonder if you did not also. When one reads such a book one asks oneself, "What does it lead to?" What does it mean to you?

Mrs. Zinno: It seems to me a going to death rather than to life.

Mr. Bacon: There is an indefinable sense of cheapness about it to me. It ends as if preparing for a sequel.

Mrs. Zinno: I think the figure of "She" is an effort to connect unreality to reality, but Antinéa remains stuck in unreality, that is, the unconscious.

Dr. Jung: You have touched upon something important there. Antinéa does not try to get out, she makes no attempt to reach the world, nor to let the world reach her. "She" is planning to rule the world, to get at it in some way. That is a peculiarity of the Anglo-Saxon, this desire to get at the world and rule it. It is quite conscious

---

[19] Either the basilica of Sacré-Cœur, on Montmarte in Paris, which had been consecrated six years earlier, and which carries a strong religious symbolism; or the Roman Catholic devotion of the Sacred Heart.

in England, and probably in fifty years will be equally so in America. But the French point of view is to remain where they are. The French are really not concerned with ruling the world, it is an affectation that Napoleon, who was not a true Frenchman, brought—i.e., the idea of dominating Europe. The French are concerned with their own country.

It is no wonder then that Antinéa sticks where she is. What I really feel about the issue is that it is hopeless. It will be repeated one hundred times, and then there is an end of the whole business. Antinéa will die, and then she will be on a throne in all her royal beauty with appropriate adornments. It is a sort of apotheosis, something one can see at the end of a film, the idea of La Gloire. There is a pantheon of fallen heroes, and there the whole thing ends in vain ambition.

Now, in *She* there is the feeling of enormous expectation at the end. One does not know, but the future is looked for. What makes a great difference between the anima of the Frenchman and that of the Anglo-Saxon is that the latter contains a mysterious side of promise, therefore there is more feeling of spiritual potencies in "She" than in Antinéa.

All that element is taken out of Antinéa by the supposition of her birth. That rational suspicion is, of course, a tremendous depreciation of the function of the archetypes. It is the "nothing but"[20] spirit again. The value is gone from the archetype. It says, "You can't base yourself on the archetypes, so it is better not to build at all, the ground is not safe." This is a peculiar fact that has to be reckoned with in the analysis of Frenchmen. It is very hard to get them to take it seriously enough. Their rationalism is blocking them at every point. They have an exact view about everything and know what it is to the last dot. They exhaust themselves in that fight. Because of this knowing how everything works, they are inclined to depreciate the immediate facts of the soul, and to assume that everything is the result of an old civilization. This was the attitude they had to take up in the Middle Ages as a compensation against the force of antiquity. Christianity was not strong enough to hold them at the beginning, and this rationalism gave support to the Church. The relation of this rationalism to the Church is something that an Anglo-Saxon can hardly understand.

[20] A term Jung took from William James: cf. "A Contribution to the Study of Psychological Types" (1913; CW 6), par. 867.

Dr. de Angulo: Will you discuss the point made in the report of the committee to the effect that Antinéa was not an unconscious figure but was put into the unconscious setting deliberately?

Dr. Jung: I think Antinéa is partly conscious and partly unconscious. When the Anglo-Saxon says she is twisted by the personal unconscious, he is commenting on the peculiar racial character of Antinéa.

Mrs. Jung: Could you say something about the relation of the animus to immortality in the same way that you discussed the anima and immortality?[21]

Dr. Jung: The animus seems to go back only to the fourteenth century, and the anima to remote antiquity, but with the animus I must say I am uncertain altogether.

Mrs. Jung: It had seemed to me that the animus was not a symbol of immortality, but of movement and life, and that it is man's attitude that gives that different aspect to the anima.

Dr. Jung: It is true that the animus is often represented by a moving figure—an aviator or a traffic manger. Perhaps there is something in the historical fact of women being more stable, therefore there is more movement in the unconscious.

Mr. Schmitz: Surely there could have been no repression of the animus at the time of the matriarchy.

Dr. Jung: We cannot be too sure.

Mrs. Zinno: The figures of gods carry the idea of immortality, do they not? Inasmuch as they are also animus figures and come into women's dreams, I should think one could say the animus carried the meaning of immortality also.

Dr. Jung: Yes, that is true, but there remains a tremendous difference between the animus and the anima.

Mr. Schmitz: Is immortality in the individual?

Dr. Jung: No, only as the image. Immortality belongs to the child of the anima. Inasmuch as the anima has not brought forth, she assumes immortality. When she brings forth she dies. But this problem of the anima and the animus is far too complex to be dealt with here.

The End

[21] Emma Jung lectured on the problem of the animus in Nov. 1931 to the Psychological Club, Zurich. The essay was published in *Wirklichkeit der Seele* (Psychologische Abhandlungen 4; Zurich, 1934); tr. C. F. Baynes, "On the Nature of the Animus," *Spring,* 1941; reprinted in E. Jung, *Animus and Anima* (New York, 1957), pp. 1–44.

ADDENDA

The following passages, not included in the transcript, are quoted in Joan Corrie, *A B C of Jung's Psychology* (London: Kegan Paul, Trench, Trubner, and New York: Frank-Maurice, [1927]), with the citation "Jung, *Lectures* (unpublished)." Other passages quoted by Corrie which do appear in the transcript are identified in the editorial notes.

(1)

Dreams being the expression of the moment must be both of the past and also leading toward a future, and therefore they cannot be understood by the causal principle alone. We can understand a process that shows developmental movement only by taking it both as a product and as an originator of something to come. I hold that psychology cannot identify with causality alone, but that we need another viewpoint as well. The system we deal with is self-regulating and so the principle of purposiveness is included in it. Particularly does the nervous system show purposive reflexes, and for that reason, anything born out of the psyche has a purposive side. . . .[1] You can push causes back indefinitely, but it is only procrastination when you do; for what matters is the present moment (Corrie, pp. 74–75).

(2)

[Corrie: ". . . at crossroads or crises on the path of life very often arresting or even awe-inspiring dreams occur. . . . This dream is"] reported by Lucius Coelius,[2] an historian of the Second Punic War, and concerns a dream of Hannibal's[3] before the undertaking of the war against Rome. Hannibal dreamed he was in an assembly of the gods themselves, not of their statues merely, and that Jupiter ordered him to undertake the war against Rome, and gave him as a guide a youth of supernatural powers, chosen from among the divine gathering.

---

[1] Ellipsis in Corrie.

[2] Lucius Coelius Antipater (fl. late 2nd cent. B.C.); other than fragments, his history of the Second Punic War is lost. Cicero recorded Coelius's account of the dream of Hannibal in *De divinatione* 1.24. Cf. M.-L. von Franz, *Dreams of Themistocles and Hannibal* (Guild of Pastoral Psychology Lecture no. 111; London, 1960), pp. 14f. / Jung mentions the dream also in the *Zarathustra* seminar, p. 498 (26 June 1935), where the editor cites Livy's history of Rome (Loeb Classical Library, V, 22) as a source.

[3] The dream is not recorded in Jung's published work.

This youth told Hannibal to follow his lead, but on no account to look back as he went. However, being unable to overcome his curiosity, Hannibal did look back and saw that what was following him was a most extraordinary monster, a sort of serpent which was wiping out of existence everything they met—houses, gardens, and woods. The interpreters said that this dream meant that he should risk the war, and that the serpent stood for the destruction of Italy. Hannibal touches the divine in his dream and is given a being with superhuman powers to be his guide. This figure has the meaning of God and expresses the superhuman element in Hannibal. That guide is to lead him into great deeds, but the divine thing is also responsible for the monster that follows.

If we take the picture presented in Hannibal's dream, first the god, then the man, then the monster, we have a fair representation of the make-up of a great man.

One could say, too, that it is just that way a great man is met in the world. People are first aware of his superior power, of his mana; then they begin to notice his human side; and finally they realize that destruction, the serpent, follows in his wake. Greatness is inevitably destructive on one side. . . .[4] To Carthage Hannibal was a Superman, but to Italy he was the destroying serpent.

The dream of Hannibal is concerned with the birth of a great deed, that is, the campaign in Italy. The fact that Hannibal hesitated to risk war showed that he was not aware of the extent of his own powers, and the unconscious had to show him his greatness. Therefore, in the words of the dream, he was called to the assembly of the gods and told by Jupiter himself what lay before him. He was given a divine guide in this undertaking because the unconscious knows what it means to follow the command of a god (Corrie, pp. 81–83).

[4] Ellipsis in Corrie.

INDEXES

1. GENERAL INDEX

166

2. CASES IN SUMMARY

In order of presentation. Cases are those mentioned by Jung, but were not necessarily treated by him.

1. H. Preiswerk, somnambulist and medium, 3–6, 9–11
2. Female psychotic who imitated shoemaking movement, 17–18
3. B. St., woman with paranoid dementia and delusions, 18–19
4. Paranoid lawyer who had attempted murder, 19
5. Young Swiss who jumped into Empress's carriage, 62–63
6. Sculptor attempting to depict Holy Ghost, 65–66
7. Woman who went insane after joining husband in Japan, 77–78
8. Wealthy patient hoping for something not grey, 78
9. Male alcoholic who saw pigs in trees, 80
10. Mother whose children "just happened," 83
11. Intuitive girl who unknowingly lived in brothel, 84
12. Intuitive patients weak on sensation, 84–85
13. Man with savior fantasy, 88–89
14. Young American whose drawings showed struggle between opposites, 101–2
15. Neurotic Austrian boy in S. America, nearly brought to murder by professor, 103
16. Divinity student doubtful about becoming a minister, 112–13
17. Man, compulsive neurotic, kept by older woman, who supposed he had analyzed his case, 125–26

3. DREAMS, FANTASIES, AND VISIONS

In order of presentation. These are dreams, and were experienced by Jung, unless otherwise noted.

1. Freud's dream on theme that Jung cannot mention, 22
2. House with multiple storeys and cellars (origin of Wandlungen u. Symbole), 22–23
3. Radiolarian, 24
4. Ghost of customs official = Freud; and Crusader, 38–39
5. Florentine loggia; white dove transformed into girl, 40
6. Fantasies of Europe in catastrophe, 41–42, 43–44
7. Fantasy: voice of woman (Spielrein?) saying his writing is art, 42, 44
8. Fantasy of digging a hole, going into a cave, fountain of blood, 47–48
9. Killing Siegfried, 48, 56–57, 61–62
10. Kekulé's vision of benzene ring, 49
11. Peter Blobb's dreams, 62
12. Visions of Elijah and Salome (on pp. 96, 99, described as dreams), 63–64, 88, 89–90, 92–99
13. Cattle bursting into cathedral during mass, 99
14. Divinity student's dream of the black and white magicians, 112–13
15. Hannibal's dream, in classical texts, 159–60

4. CHRONOLOGICAL INDEX OF
JUNG'S WORKS CITED AND DISCUSSED

The dates are of original publication or, where relevant, composition.

1896–99   *The Zofingia Lectures* (CW A), 4 n, 7 n

1902   "Zur Psychologie und Pathologie sogenannter occulter Phänomene" ("On the Psychology and Pathology of So-called Occult Phenomena"), trans. M. D. Eder, 1916 (later CW 1), 3, 5–6

1904–9   "Studies in Word Association" (CW 2), 8, 46

1906   "Psychoanalysis and Association Experiments" (CW 2), 8 n

1906   *Studies on Hysteria* (CW 4), 16 n

1907   "The Psychology of Dementia Praecox" (CW 4), 17 n, 18, 19

1908   "The Content of the Psychoses" (CW 4), 17 n, 18 n

1908   *Studies on Hysteria* (CW 4), 16 n

1912   "Neue Bahnen der Psychologie" ("New Paths in Psychology") (CW 7), vii n

1912   *Wandlungen und Symbole der Libido* (*Psychology of the Unconscious*) (tr. B. M. Hinkle, 1916), vii, viii, xii, 22–25, 26–30, 34, 38, 41 n, 67, 78, 89 n, 97 n, 98 n, 99 n, 143 n

1912   "The Theory of Psychoanalysis" (CW 4), 31 n

1913   "A Contribution to the Study of Psychological Types" (CW 6), 32 n, 78 n, 157 n

1916   La Structure de l'inconscient = The Structure of the Unconscious (CW 7): vii–viii n.

1916   *Psychology of the Unconscious.* See 1912, *Wandlungen*

1916–17   *Collected Papers on Analytical Psychology*, vii, 3 n

1917   *Die Psychologie der unbewussten Prozesse* ("*The Psychology of the Unconscious Processes*") (tr., 1917), vii

1918   "On the Psychology of the Unconscious" (CW 7), 75 n

1921   *Psychological Types* (tr. H. G. Baynes, 1923) (later CW 6), vii, xiv, 6 n, 13, 28, 30 n, 31 n, 34, 39 n, 58, 64 n, 67 n, 78, 87, 93 n, 120 n, 143 n, 149 n

1923   Polzeath Seminar, xiv

1925   Swanage Seminar, vii n

1925   "Marriage as a Psychological Relationship" (CW 17), xiii n

The Collected Works of C. G. Jung

Editors: Sir Herbert Read (d. 1968), Michael Fordham, and Gerhard Adler; executive editor, William McGuire. Translated by R.F.C. Hull (d. 1974), except vol. 2; cf. vol. 6.

* Published 1957; 2nd edn., 1970.　　　† Published 1973.

*3. THE PSYCHOGENESIS OF MENTAL DISEASE
The Psychology of Dementia Praecox (1907)
The Content of the Psychoses (1908/1914)
On Psychological Understanding (1914)
A Criticism of Bleuler's Theory of Schizophrenic Negativism (1911)
On the Importance of the Unconscious in Psychopathology (1914)
On the Problem of Psychogenesis in Mental Disease (1919)
Mental Disease and the Psyche (1928)
On the Psychogenesis of Schizophrenia (1939)
Recent Thoughts on Schizophrenia (1957)
Schizophrenia (1958)

†4. FREUD AND PSYCHOANALYSIS
Freud's Theory of Hysteria: A Reply to Aschaffenburg (1906)
The Freudian Theory of Hysteria (1908)
The Analysis of Dreams (1909)
A Contribution to the Psychology of Rumour (1910-11)
On the Significance of Number Dreams (1910-11)
Morton Prince, "The Mechanism and Interpretation of Dreams": A Critical
    Review (1911)
On the Criticism of Psychoanalysis (1910)
Concerning Psychoanalysis (1912)
The Theory of Psychoanalysis (1913)
General Aspects of Psychoanalysis (1913)
Psychoanalysis and Neurosis (1916)
Some Crucial Points in Psychoanalysis: A Correspondence between Dr. Jung and
    Dr. Loÿ (1914)
Prefaces to "Collected Papers on Analytical Psychology" (1916, 1917)
The Significance of the Father in the Destiny of the Individual (1909/1949)
Introduction to Kranefeldt's "Secret Ways of the Mind" (1930)
Freud and Jung: Contrasts (1929)

‡5. SYMBOLS OF TRANSFORMATION (1911-12/1952)
With Appendix: The Miller Fantasies

**6. PSYCHOLOGICAL TYPES (1921)
A Revision by R.F.C. Hull of the Translation by H. G. Baynes
With Four Papers on Psychological Typology (1913, 1925, 1931, 1936)

§7. TWO ESSAYS ON ANALYTICAL PSYCHOLOGY
On the Psychology of the Unconscious (1917/1926/1943)
The Relations between the Ego and the Unconscious (1928)
Appendix: New Paths in Psychology (1912); The Structure of the Unconscious
    (1916) (new versions, with variants, 1966)

* Published 1960.   † Published 1961.
‡ Published 1956; 2nd edn., 1967.   ** Published 1971.
§ Published 1953; 2nd edn., 1966.

*8. THE STRUCTURE AND DYNAMICS OF THE PSYCHE
On Psychic Energy (1928)
The Transcendent Function ([1916]/1957)
A Review of the Complex Theory (1934)
The Significance of Constitution and Heredity in Psychology (1929)
Psychological Factors Determining Human Behaviour (1937)
Instinct and the Unconscious (1919)
The Structure of the Psyche (1927/1931)
On the Nature of the Psyche (1947/1954)
General Aspects of Dream Psychology (1916/1948)
On the Nature of Dreams (1945/1948)
The Psychological Foundations of Belief in Spirits (1920/1948)
Spirit and Life (1926)
Basic Postulates of Analytical Psychology (1931)
Analytical Psychology and *Weltanschauung* (1928/1931)
The Real and the Surreal (1933)
The Stages of Life (1930-1931)
The Soul and Death (1934)
Synchronicity: An Acausal Connecting Principle (1952)
Appendix: On Synchronicity (1951)

†9. PART I. THE ARCHETYPES AND THE
COLLECTIVE UNCONSCIOUS
Archetypes of the Collective Unconscious (1934/1954)
The Concept of the Collective Unconscious (1936)
Concerning the Archetypes, with Special Reference to the Anima Concept
    (1936/1954)
Psychological Aspects of the Mother Archetype (1938/1954)
Concerning Rebirth (1940/1950)
The Psychology of the Child Archetype (1940)
The Psychological Aspects of the Kore (1941)
The Phenomenology of the Spirit in Fairytales (1945/1948)
On the Psychology of the Trickster-Figure (1954)
Conscious, Unconscious, and Individuation (1939)
A Study in the Process of Individuation (1934/1950)
Concerning Mandala Symbolism (1950)
Appendix: Mandalas (1955)

‡9. PART II. AION (1951)
    RESEARCHES INTO THE PHENOMENOLOGY OF THE SELF

**10. CIVILIZATION IN TRANSITION
The Role of the Unconscious (1918)
Mind and Earth (1927/1931)
Archaic Man (1931)
The Spiritual Problem of Modern Man (1928/1931)

* Published 1960; 2nd edn., 1969.   † Published 1959; 2nd edn., 1968.
‡ Published 1959; 2nd edn., 1968.   ** Published 1964; 2nd edn., 1970.

The Love Problem of a Student (1928)
Woman in Europe (1927)
The Meaning of Psychology for Modern Man (1933/1934)
The State of Psychotherapy Today (1934)
Preface and Epilogue to "Essays on Contemporary Events" (1946)
Wotan (1936)
After the Catastrophe (1945)
The Fight with the Shadow (1946)
The Undiscovered Self (Present and Future) (1957)
Flying Saucers: A Modern Myth (1958)
A Psychological View of Conscience (1958)
Good and Evil in Analytical Psychology (1959)
Introduction to Wolff's "Studies in Jungian Psychology" (1959)
The Swiss Line in the European Spectrum (1928)
Reviews of Keyserling's "America Set Free" (1930) and "La Révolution
    Mondiale" (1934)
The Complications of American Psychology (1930)
The Dreamlike World of India (1939)
What India Can Teach Us (1939)
Appendix: Documents (1933-1938)

*11. PSYCHOLOGY AND RELIGION: WEST AND EAST
    WESTERN RELIGION
Psychology and Religion (The Terry Lectures) (1938/1940)
A Psychological Approach to the Dogma of the Trinity (1942/1948)
Transformation Symbolism in the Mass (1942/1954)
Forewords to White's "God and the Unconscious" and Werblowsky's "Lucifer
    and Prometheus" (1952)
Brother Klaus (1933)
Psychotherapists or the Clergy (1932)
Psychoanalysis and the Cure of Souls (1928)
Answer to Job (1952)
    EASTERN RELIGION
Psychological Commentaries on "The Tibetan Book of the Great Liberation"
    (1939/1954) and "The Tibetan Book of the Dead" (1935/1953)
Yoga and the West (1936)
Foreword to Suzuki's "Introduction to Zen Buddhism" (1939)
The Psychology of Eastern Meditation (1943)
The Holy Men of India: Introduction to Zimmer's "Der Weg zum Selbst" (1944)
Foreword to the "I Ching" (1950)

†12. PSYCHOLOGY AND ALCHEMY (1944)
Prefatory note to the English Edition ([1951?] added 1967)
Introduction to the Religious and Psychological Problems of Alchemy
Individual Dream Symbolism in Relation to Alchemy (1936)
Religious Ideas in Alchemy (1937)
Epilogue

* Published 1958; 2nd edn., 1969.
† Published 1953; 2nd edn., completely revised, 1968.

*13. ALCHEMICAL STUDIES
Commentary on "The Secret of the Golden Flower" (1929)
The Visions of Zosimos (1938/1954)
Paracelsus as a Spiritual Phenomenon (1942)
The Spirit Mercurius (1943/1948)
The Philosophical Tree (1945/1954)

†14. MYSTERIUM CONIUNCTIONIS (1955-56)
AN INQUIRY INTO THE SEPARATION AND
SYNTHESIS OF PSYCHIC OPPOSITES IN ALCHEMY
The Components of the Coniunctio
The Paradoxa
The Personification of the Opposites
Rex and Regina
Adam and Eve
The Conjunction

‡15. THE SPIRIT IN MAN, ART, AND LITERATURE
Paracelsus (1929)
Paracelsus the Physician (1941)
Sigmund Freud in His Historical Setting (1932)
In Memory of Sigmund Freud (1939)
Richard Wilhelm: In Memoriam (1930)
On the Relation of Analytical Psychology to Poetry (1922)
Psychology and Literature (1930/1950)
"Ulysses": A Monologue (1932)
Picasso (1932)

**16. THE PRACTICE OF PSYCHOTHERAPY
GENERAL PROBLEMS OF PSYCHOTHERAPY
Principles of Practical Psychotherapy (1935)
What is Psychotherapy? (1935)
Some Aspects of Modern Psychotherapy (1930)
The Aims of Psychotherapy (1931)
Problems of Modern Psychotherapy (1929)
Medicine and Psychotherapy (1945)
Psychotherapy Today (1945)
Fundamental Questions of Psychotherapy (1951)
SPECIFIC PROBLEMS OF PSYCHOTHERAPY
The Therapeutic Value of Abreaction (1921/1928)
The Practical Use of Dream-Analysis (1934)
The Psychology of the Transference (1946)
Appendix: The Realities of Practical Psychotherapy ([1937] added, 1966)

§17. THE DEVELOPMENT OF PERSONALITY
Psychic Conflicts in a Child (1910/1946)

* Published 1968.   † Published 1963; 2nd edn., 1970.
‡ Published 1966.
** Published 1954; 2nd edn., revised and augmented, 1966.
§ Published 1954.

Introduction to Wickes's "Analyse der Kinderseele" (1927/1931)
Child Development and Education (1928)
Analytical Psychology and Education: Three Lectures (1926/1946)
The Gifted Child (1943)
The Significance of the Unconscious in Individual Education (1928)
The Development of Personality (1934)
Marriage as a Psychological Relationship (1925)

*18. THE SYMBOLIC LIFE
Miscellaneous Writings

†19. COMPLETE BIBLIOGRAPHY OF C. G. JUNG'S WRITINGS

†20. GENERAL INDEX TO THE COLLECTED WORKS

‡THE ZOFINGIA LECTURES
Supplementary Volume A to The Collected Works
Edited by William McGuire, translated by
Jan van Heurck, introduction by
Marie-Louise von Franz

RELATED PUBLICATIONS:

C. G. JUNG: LETTERS
Selected and edited by Gerhard Adler, in collaboration with Aniela Jaffé.
Translations from the German by R.F.C. Hull.
VOL. 1: 1906-1950
VOL. 2: 1951-1961

THE FREUD / JUNG LETTERS
Edited by William McGuire, translated by
Ralph Manheim and R.F.C. Hull

C. G. JUNG SPEAKING: Interviews and Encounters
Edited by William McGuire and R.F.C. Hull

C. G. JUNG: Word and Image
Edited by Aniela Jaffé

THE ESSENTIAL JUNG
Selected and introduced by Anthony Storr

Notes to C. G. Jung's Seminars

**DREAM ANALYSIS (1928-1930)
Edited by William McGuire

* Published 1976.
† Published 1979.
‡ Published 1983.
** Published 1984.

*NIETZSCHE'S ZARATHUSTRA (1934-1939)
Edited by James L. Jarrett (2 vols.)

†ANALYTICAL PSYCHOLOGY (1925)
Edited by William McGuire

CHILDREN'S DREAMS (1936-1941)
Edited by Lorenz Jung

* Published 1988.
† Published 1989.

PRINCETON / BOLLINGEN PAPERBACK EDITIONS

FROM THE COLLECTED WORKS OF C. G. JUNG

Aion (CW 9,ii)
Alchemical Studies (CW 13)
Analytical Psychology
Answer to Job
Archetypes and the Collective Unconscious (CW 9,i)
Aspects of the Feminine
Aspects of the Masculine
Basic Writings of C. G. Jung
The Development of Personality (CW 17)
Dreams
Essays on Contemporary Events
Essays on a Science of Mythology
The Essential Jung
Experimental Researches (CW 2)
Flying Saucers
Four Archetypes
Freud and Psychoanalysis (CW 4)
Mandala Symbolism
Mysterium Coniunctionis (CW 14)
On the Nature of the Psyche
The Practice of Psychotherapy (CW 16)
Psyche and Symbol
Psychiatric Studies (CW 1)
Psychogenesis of Mental Disease (CW 3)
Psychological Types (CW 6)
Psychology and Alchemy (CW 12)
Psychology and the East
Psychology and the Occult
Psychology and Western Religion
The Psychology of the Transference
The Spirit in Man, Art, and Literature (CW 15)
Symbols of Transformation (CW 5)
Synchronicity
Two Essays on Analytical Psychology (CW 7)
The Undiscovered Self

OTHER BOLLINGEN PAPERBACKS DEVOTED TO C. G. JUNG

C. G. Jung Speaking
Psychological Reflections
Selected Letters
C. G. Jung: Word and Image